BORN TO TAKE CHARGE

LEADERSHIP, DISCOVERY AND PURPOSE

REV. JAMES C. NYEMAH

BORN TO TAKE CHARGE

Discover Your Purpose, Reach Your Destiny

Finding the place of man in this world

[humans]

Dedication

This book is written to honor the memory of my grandfather, Pastor Peter K. Nyemah, and to salute my grandmother, Ma Phebe D. Nyemah, known as Ma Phebe of Gbiso, whose guardianship helped make me the man I am today. When I was a few days old, my grandparents took me into their home. They gave me the life of a beloved first grandson until I grew into a man. My life in Gbiso, Ma Phebe's mission, was nothing but an adventure. As a boy, I never lacked any good thing. I grew up enjoying the company of a loving family. When I look back today, I stand in gratitude for and appreciation of the fact that they gave life to the son of a teenage school girl and a runaway father.

Grandpa taught me a few practical things about life. First, to be a man, one must go to school and learn because each man becomes what he learns and profits from it. Second, one must work hard and work smart to earn a living; no food for lazy men. Finally, one woman can please a man; not so with many women. Today when I think about Grandpa, I reflect on school, hard work, and the delicate issue of women.

On the other hand, Grandma taught me spiritual things about life and ministry. To follow God, one must have complete faith in him and not lean on other things. One must have a faith that does not shrivel in the face of storms. To be accepted by God, one must come clean, surrender all, and live a holy and decent life before the Almighty. In short, Grandma taught me prayer, faith, and dedication. I love Grandma.

As I think back to my early life, I thank God so much for giving me such a great family. Grandpa and Grandma raised a great son who is now a great man of God and a leader. I am sorry that Grandpa has gone to be with the Lord, and that Grandma is of age. However, it is my prayer that I will live up to the good deposit they made into my life. I want history to show that, somehow, I made an impact. It is my prayer that God bless my grandparents as well as generations to come.

About the Author

Rev. James C. Nyemah is the first grandchild of Ma Phebe of Gbiso, a great woman of God known for prayers and miracles in Maryland County, Liberia.

He is the founder and Senior Pastor of Africa Faith Expressions, a church that touches the African community in Arizona. He is the first Liberian pastor to open a church in Phoenix. Here, some call him Brother James or Pastor James; either way, it is the same guy. He is a community man.

During the rape case of an 8-year-old Liberian girl who was molested by three boys in 2009, a story that made national and international headlines, Pastor James stood up and advocated for the family of the victim and the community.

From 2005 through 2009, his church was significantly involved in the integration process of West African refugees. To help his people, he worked with humanitarian agencies in the Valley, like the International Rescue Committee and Catholic Charities.

In 2005, Bro. James received his first degree, a B.A. in Biblical and Christian Studies with an emphasis in Inter-Cultural Ministry from Grand Canyon University. He has a distinct calling from God that directs his life.

In Arizona, he uses sports in evangelism to touch lives. He loves young people. Thanks to Rev. Nyemah, today the African community uses Cactus Park on the weekends for sports and other pastimes.

In 2008, he made his first missionary journey to Liberia, West Africa, and started three churches in rural Liberia. He has a heart for missions.

Since 2011, he has conducted several leadership conferences for pastors and community leaders all over Liberia, teaching God's word and biblical leadership, and touching 500 to 1000 pastors at a time. You can be a part of this today.

Rev. James's organization, Missions Liberia (ml), is known for leadership training and community development. He believes that good leadership and community empowerment are the best ways for Liberia to move forward.

He is working on other projects, including education, microfinance, sports, youth empowerment, and childcare programs to help rebuild Liberia.

Rev. James Nyemah and his wife, Lucy, live in Glendale, Arizona. Their daughter, Precious, is a sophomore at the University of Arizona in Tucson. Check out his first book, Where is God?, a piece about finding the place of God in this world.

Acknowledgements

I am grateful to God for Dr. John Maxwell and the Equip Team. Though we do not know each other personally, your leadership training materials have helped mold me into a leader of leaders. In December 2011, I began conducting leadership conferences in southeast Liberia and the capital of Monrovia (West Africa) with 500 to 1000 pastors and church leaders in attendance. Using the Equip materials to teach the people of God has immensely affected my life. I believe that one day we shall meet in Liberia and share time together in the Lord.

Thanks to Pastor Larrie Fraley and the Christ Church of the Valley family, who helped start Missions Liberia and our leadership conferences, using the Equip series to help pastors, church workers, and community leaders in Liberia. It gave me the opportunity to grow as a young leader. More than ever before, the people of Liberia in particular and Africa as a whole need such conferences to train leaders in the church, private sector, and public office so that they can become all that God has called them to be. Dr. Dick Stafford and the North Phoenix Baptist Church family have always been there for me as a pastor and for our church and community. I thank God for such great people, who believed in me when I first shared the vision of ministry in Arizona.

The leadership of Dr. Stafford and his church family has truly been a great help to us over the years. We bless God for such great leaders who show interest in helping emerging young leaders remain strong.

Preface

Born to Take Charge comes from the deep understanding that everything that is made has a purpose. Like man-made machinery and other inventions, all things have jobs for which they were made. Things in the natural order do have a purpose. Every day, the earth and other terrestrial bodies fulfill their purposes. The sun shines in its time; it gives light. The moon and stars guide the night. The seas and oceans play their part.

There are different seasons in a year, such as summer, autumn, winter, and spring; all of them have a purpose. The slightest variations in their timings and functions create catastrophic events for humanity.

An example of this is the Deep Freeze and Global Warming. By serving their purposes correctly, all living and nonliving things, including our planet, survive.

Vehicles are made to transport people and things. Different types of vehicles have different purposes. Microwaves, ovens, and refrigerators in our kitchens all have their purposes; even the TV remote has its own purpose. When things are used for the particular jobs for which they were made, they serve their purposes better.

Humans are not products of mere chance and the succession of atoms and molecules over millions of years. No, we are too complicated and intelligent for that. We are a creation and we have a creator; the creator made us for a purpose.

It is a purpose we must fulfill. If we do not live up to our purpose in life, life itself can be without meaning. We feel some emptiness deep within our souls; it feels like we are missing something.

We do not find contentment in people and things when we do not live in our purpose. Regardless of what we do to ignore or fill the void with other things, sadly, this longing is constant.

When we begin to live our purpose in life, it gives us some special energy to move on even in the face of our greatest opposition. The desire to fulfill our purpose, dream, or vision usually overshadows the pains and sacrifices we make to see our dreams come true.

Let me ask you today: for what do you live? I hope you are not ready to say something like "my mom," "my dad," "my love," "my kids," etc. You are not living for them. They may support you or inspire you, but your life involves more than the things you do for family and friends.

You have a purpose. It is bigger and better. If you live your life according to the whim of others, your life will have a void. I challenge you today to learn to chart the course of your own life.

If you live your life only to react to things, I encourage you today to snap out of that. Your life is much more valuable; do not let anyone control you with a remote.

When God made you, he had something better in mind. You are one of a kind. There is no one like you in all creation. Do you know that even your teeth, hair, and fingerprints are all indispensable and that there is no match for you in the whole world? Yes, that is so true.

You are one of a kind! Understanding this will bring you to self-actualization and the determination you need to discover a life of purpose.

The way you were conceived and raised has nothing to do with your purpose. If your mom was raped by some madman or armed robber, you have a purpose. If you were born behind a thatch hut in a village or in some palm tree leaves in the bathroom, you still have a purpose.

Being born in poor settings does not make you less of a person than those born in maternity centers in modern hospitals. Regardless of your origins, you have a purpose; you have a calling of God upon your life.

When you find your calling in life and begin to live your purpose, your life will have a new meaning. Please understand that just because you now know that you have a calling and purpose in life, you can sit back and expect things to orchestrate themselves; far from it!

This is the genesis of a new life of adventure. You will begin to discover what it means to live to fulfill your purpose in life. You will begin to see life in a whole new way. You have now joined millions of people around the world who, by discovering their purposes, are making great advances in the world. This is not just to their benefit, but to the benefit of humanity.

You can now begin to think like a champion. You are not a loser. You are not a "dropout." You are not useless. You have a calling.

The marketplace is waiting for you. We are waiting for your new ideas to improve on the things we already have. We want you to create new things. Step out from among your peers and become distinctive. You are peculiar. Yes, there is a path you must thread. Do not be afraid. Go on.

You are now joining the winning team. You have come to join the world of great minds, great thinkers, innovators, explorers, and adventurers.

I welcome you onboard. It is my prayer that this unit, coupled with other great resources, will help make you into the man or woman of honor you are.

You are not a mistake. You were well thought out. You were skillfully made. You were Born to Take Charge. Now go into the world and fulfill your purpose; reach your destiny.

Contents

PART ONE: #God_is_Not_Done_with_Me_Yet!
Chapter 1: My Humble Admission 17
Chapter 2: I Blundered 25

PART TWO: Sleeping at the Wrong Time
Chapter 3: While Men Slept 33
Chapter 4: Obedience Brings Victory 47
Chapter 4:1 - Obey and Learn 50
Chapter 4:2 - Know What You Learn 51
Chapter 4:3 - Apply What You Know 53
Chapter 4:4 - Build on What You Know 54
Chapter 4:5 - Excel and Be Innovative 55
Chapter 4:6 - Outgrow What You Learned 56
Chapter 4:7 - Create Your Signature Series 57
Chapter 5: Apply Your Mind 58

PART THREE: Drop the Stuff!
Chapter 6: Stinking Thinking 69
Chapter 7: Stupid Friends 78
Chapter 8: Bad Places 81
Chapter 9: Extra Load 84

PART FOUR: Born to Take Charge
Chapter 10: Five-Fold Duty Charge 91
Chapter 11: Born to Bear Fruit 95
Chapter 12: Born to Multiply 102
Chapter 13: Born to Fill the Earth 106
Chapter 14: Born to Subdue 110
Chapter 15: Born to Have Dominion 120

PART FIVE: Pray Hard and Work Hard
Chapter 16: Faith - The God Factor 133
Chapter 17: Work - The Human Factor 135
Chapter 18: Prayer Changes Things 139

PART SIX: Wait!
Chapter 19: Waiting is Not Doing Nothing 153
Chapter 20: Waiting Prepares Us 155
Chapter 21: Waiting Gives Us Knowledge 158
Chapter 22: Waiting Instills Character 160
Chapter 23: Waiting Brings Rewards 162

PART SEVEN: Connecting the Dots
Chapter 24: You Cannot Do It Alone 171
Chapter 25: We Need God! 174

PART EIGHT: #Fix_Me_Up
Chapter 26: I am Not a Mistake 181
Chapter 27: I Have a Purpose 184
Chapter 28: Take Charge 191

PART ONE:
#God_is_Not_Done_with_Me_Yet!

Not always do we see people ready to admit their wrongs publicly, especially by writing those wrongs in a book that will last for years. When I look back at everything that has happened in my life, I think it is better to come to a humble admission and make a confession.

Some people tried to convince me not to do this, but I think it is a necessary part of my growth and development. I understand that I cannot be ashamed of my past and keep it as some secret to haunt me forever; no.

It is for this reason that I have come to understand that I have not been all I need to be. I admit that I blundered, yet I know another thing—God is not done with me yet.

- My Humble Admission
- I Blundered

Chapter 1: My Humble Admission

I may not be great like you; compared to others, I may be nothing. But one thing I know is that God is Not Done with Me Yet! Perhaps my parents envisioned more from me than what I am today.

I am sorry. Please tell them to hold their peace because all hope is not lost. Tell my grade-school teachers and university professors—who have not yet have seen the great headlines that they expected about me—to wait a moment. I am coming.

Tell my wife that I am sorry for not being the type of husband she wanted to boast about; please tell her to give me just a little more time. She knows that I can do better.

Please tell my kids that I know they deserve better; tell them to give Daddy some time and things will work out. Please relate this to my church and community: I may be far away from who I am supposed to be, but I know that through me God can do great things for them. I am working on it; tell them not to give up on me so soon. I am coming.

Please tell all of them that "God is Not Done with Me Yet!" I may be in a mess that seems unredeemable, but tell them not to lose hope in me altogether. I am taking steps in the right direction. I am coming.

Please tell my friends that I know we have come from afar; I am working on my act. Very soon I will make a great friend, one to whom all of them will be proud to be connected. I am coming.

I know by now you may be wondering, "Why is he giving apologies to all these people and how does it connect to anything here? Why all these apologies with little hope of redemption in the end?" Well, before I answer that, I want you to complete a little exercise.

Go back to the beginning of this chapter and read it as though it were you speaking. Now consider all the references as though they were to your parents, spouse, kids, teachers, friends, organizations, and community—as though it were you directly speaking those words to them.

If you have done that, here is a question for you. Do you in any way feel that you have failed any of them during your lifetime?

Have you ever failed your parents, spouse, kids, organization, community, or friends? If you answer "yes" to any of these, you are like me.

We all need to know that just because we have failed in some areas, our lives are not over. At least not yet because we still have a chance to redeem the time.

If you answered "no" to all of these categories of people, I hope you are not lying; this is not a test to pass for a grade. But if your answer is an honest "no," then I thank God for you because you are a decent, moral and perhaps pious person; you are actually one of a kind. Many of us who have failed people in our lifetime are not proud of it, but sadly that is the truth.

Now let me ask you: If you are a parent and if your kid is acting out and doing bad things, would you give up on him or her just like that? For you married couples, would you give up on your spouse if you sensed that he or she was doing something wrong without trying to fix things?

To the teachers, do you not have hope that your pupils will advance in life and do something wonderful with what they have learned from you? It is true that we sometimes write off people as "useless," "good for nothing," "dropouts," and "total failures" just because they make mistakes.

Let us have hope in them that they can do better. We, too, are in a way saying that we believe that God is not done with them yet. I think we are saying the same thing now.

So why was I giving out apologies? I believe that in my short lifetime I have failed some people, including those I listed. In spite of that, I have come to my senses and now recognize my own situation, about which I need to do something. Due to the complexity of this effort, I must ask all the people I know to bear with me and give me some time, as God is working on me.

I believe I have great potential. I believe I have something that can make life worthwhile. I have dreams and visions that will benefit not only my family and me, but also others.

I am now working with God to fix myself up. Just like many of you, I want to be a better child to my parents, a darling spouse, a loving father, a wonderful coworker, a dependable friend, a trustworthy community leader, and a morally decent person.

Because of this I began working with God to surrender all to him. I told God to fix my mind because it really needs a lot of work. Instead of thinking about great and principled things, I found that my thoughts are not all that good. I told God to fix my heart because from my heart my mouth speaks. It always gets me into unwanted trouble.

Two other things I took the time to talk to God about are my feelings and emotions. They can get out of control so fast, before I even realize it. I get angry and do things that aren't necessary. I feel this way and that way about people. The truth is, many times I am wrong.

Besides that, my feelings and emotions long for pleasures outside of what I already have or should have. It should not be that way; I should at least be happy with what I have.

Please let me say one last thing before I bore you with this long list; I think it will interest you. It is about my eyes and my imagination. I see things. I imagine things. To be frank, I do not think I should even tell you what my eyes like to see and my mind likes to imagine; it is just too deep.

Because of all these things, I really had to talk to God and ask him to help me. It was not about religiosity; I just needed God. It's interesting to think that, contrary to how many so-called Christians and moral people would label me (and I believe they would reject people like me), God actually visited me. That was when he told me that he is not done with me yet.

Instead of the harsh hate messages and condemnations and threats of hellfire that I heard from preachers everywhere—preachers who seemed to be bereft of love and patience for the sinner—God showed me undeserved love.

I was surprised that such an entity—one that religious people, especially Christians, talk about, this divine God—would come down to my level. It made me doubt whether many Christians actually know God and his love.

I do not know, but they seem to present God to people from a place of fear and guilt instead of relating a simple, clear message of his acceptance, love, and hope for sinners and underperformers. People respond to fear.

In that meeting, God reminded me how he made me and what he made me for. He told me about the power and authority that accompanies the responsibility he conferred upon me. It was something I had never known before. He even said that he made the animals to respect me; that was so cool.

The writer of Genesis said this as he reminded us that, in the beginning, God said,

[1]*"Let us make mankind in our image, in our likeness, so that they may rule over the fish in the sea and the birds in the sky, over the livestock and all the wild animals, and over all the creatures that move along the ground."*

So God created mankind in his own image, in the image of God he created them; male and female he created them.

God blessed them and said to them, "Be fruitful and increase in number; fill the earth and subdue it. Rule over the fish in the sea and the birds in the sky and over every living creature that moves on the ground.

[2]*The fear and dread of you will fall on all the beasts of the earth, and on all the birds in the sky, on every creature that moves along the ground, and on all the fish in the sea; they are given into your hands."*
[Genesis 1:26-28]

This is good stuff. If I was made in grand style for a purpose, was given some huge responsibilities, and am equipped for the job, why am I living in such a mess? Now I have come to my senses. I am better than this.

As we began to converse, I was told more things about myself that I did not know. God revealed deep, secret things no one knew about. He told me about my potential, highlighted my strengths, and talked mildly about my weaknesses.

I have made some mistakes in life. God said that he will work with me in spite of my errors. He promised to work with me in a very special way and to make me into something more spectacular, something people will demand.

As a matter of fact, God told me that he would take me to the potter's house to break me, mold me, and make me over. I have no idea how it is going to be because I have not been there before. Yet I can tell you that, since our first meeting, I no longer have an interest in some of the things I did before; some habits are leaving me. What also surprised me is that some people I thought were good are also leaving me in this cleansing process.

I now understand that not everything is good for me. Not all the people out there, with all their good intentions, are supposed to be close to me. Not even all the places I went are good for me. God is removing some of them from my life.

I love this, but it is painful to lose some people to whom I am so accustomed. I must suppress that emotion and work with God because he knows what is good for me. As difficult as this process is, I do believe that when God is done with me I will be better off than I am now. God is Not Done with Me Yet!

I must say this to God: I thank you, God, I thank you, father; I know you love me so much and expect so much of me for the life, people, and things you have given me. I am sorry I misused some of them. I failed.

I must say thank you for your undeserved grace upon my life; for daily provision, protection, connections; and for letting me know you better. You are not like those religious freaks who want to shove religion down my throat by force. Thank you.

The fact that I am still alive gives me the hope I need to continue in life despite my situation. I thank you, God, for where I am right now; perhaps there are many others who want to be like me.

I know I am in a place where you can find me and save me; thank you for where I am. I am coming. I am coming. We are in this together. Every day gets better; I know more and more that you are not done with me yet. There is a better me that is yet to be revealed. Thank you. This is my solemn prayer.

Now you are getting a deeper understanding of why this piece is so important. Perhaps you need to try God so that he can begin working to make a better you. I believe your parents, spouse, kids, friends, colleagues, organization, and community expect more of you, too.

Why not ask God to make you a little better than you are today? I think it would be a good choice. If God does not work for you, continue in your ways; it is that simple.

God is Not Done with Me Yet! comes from knowing the love of God. I am beginning to know his grace; it is a gift from God to humankind, and something so undeserved. It says that people like me still qualify for his grace.

It is a blessed assurance that there is still room at the cross for someone like me. I am glad to know that God can fix me up in his love, grace, and mercy. I feel good. The Gospel of John states that,

³Out of his fullness we have all received grace in place of grace already given. [John 1:16]

I also learned from the Apostle Paul that God said,

⁴My grace is sufficient for you, for my power is made perfect in weakness. [I Corinthians 12:9]

If grace helps me make it in life, then I really need extra grace. I need grace every day because I want to move forward in life. Grace is accepting, understanding, and forgiving. It has hope.

I understand that the love of God is still available for someone like me. Regardless of all I have done and where I am today, God still loves me.

Wow, that is so wonderful. It is good to know that God does not love only good, moral, pious, or Christian people. He loves weaklings and poor performers and underperformers. God loves the rich and mighty just as he loves the poor and needy. He loves everybody.

The writer John said of the love of God,

⁵ Greater love has no one than this: to lay down one's life for one's friends. [John 1:13]

If God can come down to my level, I must respond in kind.

I now know about the mercy of God. The mercy of God is renewed every morning for me. This stuff is good. The Prophet Jeremiah had hope in the mercy and love of God when he said,

⁶The faithful love of the LORD never ends! His mercies never cease. Great is his faithfulness; his mercies begin afresh each morning.
[Lamentations 3:22-23]

This is all good news for everybody, including people like me who need to be fixed up. It gives hope. It tells me that God is faithful; his love is constant. His mercies are never-ending and are new every morning.

They are not leftovers from yesterday, but fresh for today—just what I need because of my condition. It is important for me to have new mercies daily because, as humans, our grace and mercy have a way of expiring quickly.

When we begin to list examples of our "lavish grace and mercy" to others, we are on the verge of cutting it off. It is saying that yesterday I helped. Yesterday I forgave you. Today is a new day and I cannot keep helping you all the time. Yet God gives new mercies on a daily basis. He gives his mercy free of charge. I thank God for his love, mercy, and grace.

This tells me that once I have life, God has a plan for me and that is why he is keeping me alive. I was Born to Take Charge, so I cannot allow myself to remain this way. It makes me recognize my problems and brings me to an honest admission that I need a savior.

To declare that "God is Not Done with Me Yet!" is to come to my senses, to realize that I was once something I no longer am or that I have hope of becoming something I am not yet. Either way, I recognize that God is the one who can make it happen for me against all odds.

I am eternally grateful to God for where I am today. Lord, I realize that I have a long way to go in terms of knowing you and your purpose for my life.

I understand that I may be a little difficult to deal with, but because of your unconditional love, daily mercies, and sufficient grace, I know I can make it. In my moment of weakness, I am covered by your grace.

I do not brag about receiving this wonderful gift of love, mercy, and grace because I want to continue in my ways. I want to make progress in life. I want to join those who are doing something better with their lives.

I want to be a child who brings honor to my parents. I want to be a spouse who makes my partner feel as though she made the right decision in life by being with me. I want my kids to call me a wonderful dad. I want all my friends to see the champion in me.

I want to give back to my community, to speak justice and bring about social change. I want my organization to know that I am a great asset and that they are lucky to have me.

I want to be better than what I currently am. I know that God_Is_Not_Done_with_Me_Yet! I know that quite well. I have now come to understand more than ever before that I have a purpose in my life.

I cannot live my life any way I want. I have a dream. I have a purpose. I am a good and dependable contributor to life and to my country. I have now come to understand that there is something special about me, so I cannot allow my life to waste away due to laziness, slothfulness, or addiction to drugs, alcohol, or sex. No, that is not my portion. I am better than that!

I admit that I am not perfect. Please do not push me into perfection before I frustrate you because I do not claim any perfection. Instead, I now know how to live a decent, moral life. I can claim righteousness by doing what is right.

Let me take a quick break and say this to you: Whether you are spiritual, religious, or even an atheist, you, too, can put your life together. Everyone needs love, mercy, and grace. You will reap these rewards when you decide to move forward with your life, and you will have nothing to lose except for your bad habits.

Sorry for the diversion; we can continue now. As for me, I want to cling to what is good, to what is noble, to what will put smiles on the faces of people I meet. I want to do something good with my life. I do all this because I was Born to Take Charge! Today I make the pledge to take charge of my life; so help me, God.

Chapter 2: I Blundered

I want to talk about the reality of life for many people. As we proceed through this section, remember these words: hope, courage, and redemption. I believe that many of us can admit that we have blundered at some point in our lives.

We made a mess somewhere. We failed in small ways and we failed in big ways. Many of us carry the scars of our weaknesses; some people have physical scars on their bodies. Many of us carry deep-rooted emotional and mental scars that bother us to this day.

The truth is that nobody is perfect; we are pruned to make mistakes that hurt us and other people. There are times when, through our blunders we hurt people who are dear to us.

Whether it was out of anger, fear, frustration, or revenge, we hurt people. The feeling of remorse can be draining. Even if we did it under the influence of drugs or alcohol, we are not exempted from the consequences. When we come to our senses, we can find it frightening to discover what we have done. It puts us in a place where we must decide whether or not to fix the situation.

There are some people who can really plot evil to hurt others. They plan quite well, rehearse, and then go out to implement their plans. Whether these plans are on a large scale or small scale, the act of scheming to hurt others is not good at all; we must resist such lifestyles.

When we have failed in terms of morality and do evil things, we must understand that we can stop. There is a way out.

I think it would be difficult to believe anyone who claims that he or she has not blundered, failed, or hurt anyone in any way. I believe that, one way or another, all of us have failed people. When we have blundered, we need to try to fix the problem and not allow time to pass.

Time has a way of making matters worse. Many people do not necessarily forget, and time makes the problem grow.

Unresolved matters between two people have a way of involving others. If we are not careful, the situation turns into a dangerous family-versus-family revenge saga. On a large scale, wars erupt and people seek to destroy each other for something that could have been settled in homes, over round tables, or between hallways.

Let me tell you a story that will remind you of the few words I told you to remember: hope, courage, and redemption. It is a story of greed, love, abuse of power, murder, harsh discipline, and redemption. This is the story of King David of Israel and Bathsheba.

[7]In the spring, at the time when kings go off to war, David sent Joab out with the king's men and the whole Israelite army. They destroyed the Ammonites and besieged Rabbah. But David remained in Jerusalem.

One evening David got up from his bed and walked around on the roof of the palace. From the roof he saw a woman bathing. The woman was very beautiful, and David sent someone to find out about her. The man said, "She is Bathsheba, the daughter of Eliam and the wife of Uriah the Hittite." Then David sent messengers to get her. She came to him, and he slept with her. (Now she was purifying herself from her monthly uncleanness.) Then she went back home. The woman conceived and sent word to David, saying, "I am pregnant."

So David sent this word to Joab: "Send me Uriah the Hittite." And Joab sent him to David. When Uriah came to him, David asked him how Joab was, how the soldiers were and how the war was going. Then David said to Uriah, "Go down to your house and wash your feet."

So Uriah left the palace, and a gift from the king was sent after him. But Uriah slept at the entrance to the palace with all his master's servants and did not go down to his house.

David was told, "Uriah did not go home." So he asked Uriah, "Haven't you just come from a military campaign? Why didn't you go home?"

Uriah said to David, "The ark and Israel and Judah are staying in tents, and my commander Joab and my lord's men are camped in the open country. How could I go to my house to eat and drink and make love to my wife? As surely as you live, I will not do such a thing!"

Then David said to him, "Stay here one more day, and tomorrow I will send you back." So Uriah remained in Jerusalem that day and the next.

At David's invitation, he ate and drank with him, and David made him drunk. But in the evening Uriah went out to sleep on his mat among his master's servants; he did not go home. In the morning David wrote a letter to Joab and sent it with Uriah.

In it he wrote, "Put Uriah out in front where the fighting is fiercest. Then withdraw from him so he will be struck down and die."

So while Joab had the city under siege, he put Uriah at a place where he knew the strongest defenders were.

When the men of the city came out and fought against Joab, some of the men in David's army fell; moreover, Uriah the Hittite died. After the time of mourning was over, David had her brought to his house, and she became his wife and bore him a son.

But the thing David had done displeased the LORD. [II Samuel 11:1-16, 27]

King David had about seven wives in Hebron during his seven years' reign there, and one listed wife in Jerusalem during his thirty-three years' reign there. If in seven years he married seven wives, one can only imagine how many women he married in thirty-three years.

Interestingly, the king had many other unlisted wives and concubines between Hebron and Jerusalem. Even with all these women, who varied in terms of beauty, size, and performance, King David still wanted his soldier's wife. This is ridiculous.

Why would the king bring himself down like this? Well, when we are about to get in trouble, our rational minds suspend good thinking; our feelings and emotions take over. Such was the case with King David.

The king blundered in a big way. He acted lazy. During a time when kings went to war, he stayed home, sending General Joab instead. With plenty of free time, the king began to wander; while wandering he saw a naked woman bathing.

Instead of acting "royal" and avoiding the sight, he continued looking until he became infatuated with her; he lusted after her. He acted out his evil desires and lust by sending for her and convincing her to go to bed with him even though the Law of Moses forbade adultery.

The king and the lady knew that the penalty for their act was death, yet the two proceeded with an extramarital affair. Were they trying to commit suicide or what? Or was the lady carried away by the charm of the king and thinking that their actions would not be condemned because they involved the king himself?

Perhaps the king urged her to do it because of his position, but they forgot that there was another leader in Israel whom no one could mess with—Prophet Nathan. Prophet Nathan was a force to reckon with because, as a man of God, he carried the power of God.

As a matter of fact, King David took orders from him before he could commit the army to war. Prophet Nathan was the spiritual leader of the nation of Israel. However, when sin threatens, we tend to forget the heavy price we pay for it. Bathsheba forgot; King David forgot. Forgetfulness is a terrible thing.

When we forget good things, we suffer embarrassment. To avoid trouble, we should never forget important things. Because David forgot that there was another leader over him, he abused his kingship to take another man's wife. That didn't go well for him in the end.

Bathsheba forgot that even though her new lover, King David, spared her life for the adultery charge, because he was also a culprit, the law could still catch her. Reasoning like that could not stand before the "no-nonsense" prophet.

Sin has a way of blinding us and corrupting our minds. It deceives and leads us into nothing but trouble and death—physical, spiritual, and emotional death.

Bathsheba got punished for committing adultery; God killed her baby. King David also received a harsh punishment for his crime. The child died and many other things happened.

His son Amnon raped his daughter; when David did not carry out the Law of Moses against the offender, his other son, Absalom, took matters into his own hands and killed his brother. Trouble began to enter King David's house. He killed a man by the sword; his son killed his other son by the sword.

After some time, his son, Absalom, who had a disloyal and rebellious spirit, formed a faction to overthrow his father. When the king heard that his son was bringing an army against him, he ran barefoot out of the palace. Absalom drank from the king's cup and slept with the king's wives, who had been left behind.

King David was publicly disgraced and mocked. A civil war broke out between the army of Absalom and King David's army; in the end, Absalom was killed. King David mourned the death of his son as the nation mourned the dead members of the army—all because of one little act of illegal sex.

Many of us commit fornication and adultery without any problem; some of us do it over and over again without conscience. Yet because King David slept with a woman who did not belong to him, he and his country faced a lot of problems. A good soldier was murdered. A baby died. A daughter was raped, two princes died, civil war broke out, and the king was disgraced and mocked.

I do not think it was worth it at all. I am not here to judge King David, as I have my own problems. Yet we can learn something from this—we must prevent such things from happening to us.

It is so easy to see the problems of other people and become blind to our own problems (which might be worse than those of others). We all have issues. King David had a woman problem. He had a problem with disciplining his children. He compromised the Law of Moses even though his son was guilty.

In the end, after the death of his rebellious son Absalom, King David reigned until he appointed his young son Solomon to succeed him. King David had the grace to overcome his problems; not all of us get this type of fairytale ending. We should not take joy in the negative things that others experience, but rather let them serve as lessons that will prevent us from facing similar or worse problems. Life is very interesting. Some people can do certain things and get away with them, but this is not so for everyone. Some of us get caught or get into serious trouble.

I do not know what your strengths and weaknesses are, but please be careful. Do not allow your feelings and emotions to lead you astray and compel you to do something that will embarrass you and the people you know. We are not perfect, but we can make up our minds to be better.

We can agree to stop thinking about certain things. We can let go of certain people who assert a bad influence upon our lives. We can stop going to places where we find ourselves tempted to do bad things. We can learn to control our mouths and our thoughts.

When we do this, with the help of family, friends, coworkers, and fellow church members, we are on the path to progress. We can start from where we are and do something meaningful with our lives. We must refuse to negatively classify people, as we are better than that. We can turn our lives into an ever-forward, never-turning mode. God bless you.

PART TWO:
Sleeping at the Wrong Time

As good as sleep is, sleeping at the wrong time can disorient us, make us forget important things, and let trouble overtake us.

I understand that sleep is an essential part of our natural existence. Sleeping too much is a problem, yet sleeping too little can be a problem as well. Therefore, we must have a unique balance of work, play, eat, and sleep for our bodies to function properly.

Follow me as I discuss the issue of sleeping at the wrong time. Perhaps you will discover that some of the problems that affect your life, family, business, or church stem from the fact that you are sleeping at the wrong time.

We should not sleep at the wrong time when there are things to take care of. When we sleep at the wrong time, we give evil people opportunities to mess with our stuff. It is still day; wake up.

Chapter 3: While Men Slept

We all know that,

⁸There is a time for everything, and a season for every activity under the heavens. [Ecclesiastes 3:1]

So it is with sleep.
King Solomon of Israel said it right when he talked about times and seasons; everything has its own time and season. When things are done in their proper times and seasons, they can better fulfill their purposes; otherwise, there will be a problem. We all know that sleep is good; regardless of our tight schedules and the enormity of our work, we must make time for sleep. When we do not sleep as required, our performances are affected and our bodies are strained. It could also lead to more serious problems. In short, sleep is good; we should all get proper sleep.

When we sleep, we rest from our day's work and allow our bodies to recuperate, thereby giving them more functionality. The psalmist said that,

⁹In peace I will lie down and sleep, for you alone, Lord, make me dwell in safety. [Psalm 4:8]

When we sleep we become vulnerable, but the Lord becomes our safety. The writer of Proverbs talks about the assurance the Lord provides when we sleep. He said,

¹⁰When you lie down, you will not be afraid; when you lie down, your sleep will be sweet." [Proverbs 3:24]

This is good to hear—that fear will not be our portion when we sleep. We will not think about what wicked people might do and we won't worry so much; instead, our sleep will be good and sweet. We need to sleep in peace and enjoy the process. We give our bodies good rest and energy for the next day.

Interestingly, there is a problem when we sleep too much.

Sleep is good, but sleeping too much is bad.

Sleeping at the wrong time is bad; it is dangerous for us. Sleeping at a time when we should be doing something meaningful is a terrible thing. Jesus, in trying to make his audience understand his message about the kingdom of God, said that,

[11]The kingdom of heaven is like a man who sowed good seed in his field. But while everyone was sleeping, his enemy came and sowed weeds among the wheat, and went away. When the wheat sprouted and formed heads, then the weeds also appeared.

The owner's servants came to him and said, "Sir, didn't you sow good seed in your field? Where then did the weeds come from?" "An enemy did this," he replied.

The servants asked him, "Do you want us to go and pull them up?"

"No," he answered, "because while you are pulling the weeds, you may uproot the wheat with them. Let both grow together until the harvest. At that time I will tell the harvesters: "First collect the weeds and tie them in bundles to be burned; then gather the wheat and bring it into my barn." [Matthew 13:24-30]

In this parable, a man sowed good seeds in his farm, but while everyone was sleeping his enemy came and sowed weeds (bad seeds) among the good seeds.

The enemy corrupted his farm. The good work was tarnished. The man's money and hard work were affected; his rights were violated while he and his servants slept. His hope for a harvest was affected; his resources for the future would be limited. His operations would be adversely affected because his enemy sowed bad seeds in his farm of good seeds. While the enemy was busy working overtime to corrupt and destroy his farm, the man and his servants slept, only to wake up to the troubling news about the work of his enemy.

It appears as though the farmer forgot that he had an enemy, or perhaps he underestimated his enemy. It could also be that he was familiar with the enemy, but overlooked the enemies' tactics and miscalculated his moves. He planted his farm, but left it without security even though he knew he had an enemy who would use any opportunity to destroy him.

Jesus reminds us about the enemy and calls him a thief when he says,

^{12}The thief comes only to steal and kill and destroy; I have come that they may have life, and have it to the full. [John 10:10]

I want you to bear with me as I deal with the horrific issue of sleeping, carelessness, corruption, and wickedness in some places across the globe. This reminds me of the problem in the continents of Africa and South America, but most especially Africa.

Somebody has been stealing from Africa.

Africa is one of the richest continents in the world, full of natural resources like diamonds, gold, iron ore, bauxite and other fine minerals, oil in land and deep waters, rich biodiversity, plant and animal life, and land naturally fertilized for plantations. Yet it is the poorest and most troubled place on planet earth! Why? Africa, why?

Africa has everything it needs to be self-sufficient and to prosper without aid from the West! God blessed Africa so much that its land can support and sustain its citizenry. Quite interestingly, history has proven that the natural endowments of Africa have attracted thieves and lords of wars. They have taken Africa hostage. Please save Africa.

Please excuse me, but I must ask a few questions here. Why does the rich continent of Africa have no food for its citizens? Why is there a lack of good security for our countries? Why is there no cheap cement, nor even iron and steel for our construction projects, when iron ore is mined in Africa? Why is it that the oil and fine minerals in the earth and waters in America and other Western countries do not cause civil wars or riots, which are commonplace in Africa? Something is not right; something is terribly wrong. We, the people of Africa, must step up to the challenge and fix the problem before it's too late.

Africa has not truly discovered its own value yet. Out of Africa's own self-ambitions in times past, we have waged wars against our own brothers and treated each other poorly. The West discovered us and scornfully invested in our own wicked passions, leading to a situation in which thousands upon thousands of African slaves were carried away to Europe and America so that they could work in plantation labor camps.

But that's not the only thing; envious of the development of the black man, some people and countries fought hard to destroy every good thing about the continent and its people. They destroyed cities and cultures and any cultural artifacts that spoke of the real history of Africa. In their arrogance and pride, they manipulated the people of Africa, scornfully rewrote their true history, hid their true identities, destroyed anything that spoke of the truth, and introduced false institutions and systems to keep the people down as they looted the land.

Even though slavery ended, a new type of slavery was created to benefit certain groups. After emancipation, the next and current phase has been corruption and plunder. Oppressing groups always find ways to dupe the black man and enrich themselves, even if it means starting conflicts between political parties with the sole purpose of creating a war that gives them an excuse to sell guns and other munitions while they loot the land. Many times, they have ulterior motives as they laugh, pretending to do business, offering aid, or trying to be friends. We have seen in many cases that, if there is no special interest, they do not go anywhere to offer help unless circumstances compel them to do so.

It seems like the West is telling Africa,

"Since you Africans are stupid, we took your people for slaves; now, we are taking your stuff."

Why does Africa need continual aid from the West—a situation that creates dependency—when the continent can underwrite its own projects and care for its own people? The answer is simple. A seed of distrust and corruption has been sown and is flourishing well among the people of Africa.

Many African leaders trust Westerners more than they trust each other. Nowadays, the common people have also learned not to trust their leaders—and definitely not to trust each other.

The educated West has shown Africans how to outsmart and cheat each other; as they do that, the West siphons all the good stuff, leaving only pocket change for African leaders to squander.

Without realizing it, African leaders have been stealing from their countries and serving the interests of the West, leaving the rich continent full of nothing but abject poverty, sickness, and a lack of development.

Sadly, when you leave Africa and travel to any Western country, you'll notice a vast difference between the place and people in terms of development. This is so sickening.

How can Africans not see this conspiracy—that some special interest groups are keeping things the way they are so that they can enrich themselves and exert influence and power over us?

A significant number of African nations are on the World's Top 100 Corrupt Countries list, and Africa is constantly riddled with wars, famine, and disease. Africa has more poor countries than any other place in the world. Why is Africa rich but poor?

I am so hurt every time I think about all the smart, educated, talented, and religious people in Africa who are treated as free labor for Americans and Europeans. Now the Chinese have crossed the seas to take their portion. What is going on, people of Africa? When will we wake from our sleep?

Why do you sleep and let others sterilize your women and infect your people with various diseases under the guise of vaccines? After some of you learn what development is, how can you not develop your own home? Why don't you become the change you want to see? Where are the intellectuals and educated people? Are they sleeping, too? Africans must wake up to the dawning of a new day, a day of hope for us and our children. Ladies and gentlemen, we must arise!

From the savannahs in Ethiopia to the safari in Kenya and Botswana, and to the Niger delta in Nigeria; then to the Nile valley in Egypt, and on to the tropical rainforest in Liberia and Victoria Falls in Zimbabwe, there must be smart, educated, and intelligent people full of integrity in Africa. We must wake up and do something before it is too late.

It seems as though, as a people, we have been sleeping while the West plundered our land. As a man, it hurts me to see them taking our women and our possessions. If they took our people in the past and are now taking our possessions, what is next? Sell the continent or what? This is so unfair!

I am left to wonder about the place of the Church in Africa. Is the Church, like many African leaders, affected by cheap politics, competition, personal glory, and material goods?

Where is the Church in Africa? Where is the Church that is so full of the power and anointing of God? Where is the Church we hear around every street corner across the continent? Where is the Church where night prayers filled the darkest skies? Where is the Church where bells ring every Sunday morning? Where is the Church that should stand for God and declare the word of God against the injustices that occur on its doorsteps?

Is the Church in Africa good only for performing miracles on Sundays—healing the sick and saving a few souls—or can God work in us for transformation and profound leadership to govern our land and its people?

To the Church in Africa, God says,

[13]*Arise, shine; for your light has come! And the glory of the Lord is risen upon you.* [Isaiah 60:1]

I say, arise and shine for it is time to allow God to manifest his "kingdom come" in Africa. God does not delight in injustices, corruption, and other human sufferings like sickness, poverty, bad leadership, and a poor church with no impact on the land. Let the Church in Africa arise and stand against the intrusion of the enemy.

I have come to realize that God does not just want to see us saved and experience healing. He does not want to simply give us a few provisions so that we can live from hand to mouth. God wants us to take charge of the land.

God wants to see neighborhoods and cities transformed. He wants to see countries transformed, to have law and order and justice served without sentiment. God wants to see businesses grow and great advances made in education. He wants human development and capacity building because we are behind the rest of the world. God wants the best for us. He does not want us to be liable to anyone. We have what it takes to make this happen, but we must open our eyes and guide our hearts accordingly.

The enemy is tactical; we need to be mindful and act accordingly if we want to move forward.

The writer of Proverbs talks about sleep, sluggishness, and laziness when he asked,

[14]How long will you lie there, you sluggard? When will you get up from your sleep? A little sleep, a little slumber, a little folding of the hands to rest—and poverty will come on you like a thief and scarcity like an armed man. [Proverbs 6:9-11]

There is a serious question we must all answer; the way we answer it determines our course of action. How long will we sleep while trouble is coming? How long will we fold our hands and close our eyes while everything is going wrong?

We must arise. We must unfold our hands and wake to the dawning of a new day. We must not sleep and let the vices of life take over. We must not sleep and let the wicked and corrupt people take over our land, take our wives and children, and take our property. We must not sleep and let illiteracy, poverty, injustice, famine, and disorder engulf our society. A new day has dawned; every sleeper must awake from his or her slumber. Wake up because it is time to work.

Matthew, the writer of the first book in the New Testament, talks about how the disciples betrayed Jesus when he needed them the most. It was the night of his arrest when he went to the garden to pray. Jesus wanted his disciples to pray with him, but sadly they were all sleeping. Here is the account:

[15]Going a little farther, he fell with his face to the ground and prayed, "My Father, if it is possible, may this cup be taken from me. Yet not as I will, but as you will."

Then he returned to his disciples and found them sleeping.

"Couldn't you men keep watch with me for one hour?" he asked Peter.

"Watch and pray so that you will not fall into temptation. The spirit is willing, but the flesh is weak." [Matthew 26:39-41]

I cannot imagine how terrible Jesus must have felt when at the time he needed his disciples the most—to keep watch and pray—they were all sleeping, and not just one time, but three times!

Let me ask you this simple question: To whom did you make a promise that you failed to keep? Please do not be quick to say "nobody." I believe that when you look deeper in your heart, you will remember a time and place where you gave your word to somebody but you never fulfilled it. I think you can remember something now.

I believe all of us have failed others—including those closest to us—in many ways without realizing how negatively our actions affected them. Just because they were nice and said that it was okay does not mean that the situation really was alright. The truth is that we promised them and later lied to them. That is not cool at all.

I do not like people who make promises, then break them without a second thought. I actually think nobody would say that he or she likes being lied to, or that they like people who are not dependable. I do not think so. We all must be careful; we cannot be sleeping when we are supposed to be there for our friends and family.

When we sleep during a time when we are supposed to be busy working to fulfill our promises, it speaks negatively about us.

Our actions tell others that we are untrustworthy; we cannot be counted on. When we do this, we could lose good friends and opportunities, so we must be careful. The result of this is nothing but loneliness, shame, and disgrace.

When people sleep at the wrong time, they can be corrupted without even knowing it.

At one time during the journey of the Israelites in the wilderness, God told Moses,

16Go down from here at once, because your people whom you brought out of Egypt have become corrupt. They have turned away quickly from what I commanded them and have made an idol for themselves. [Deuteronomy 9:12]

The children of Israel suffered in captivity for many years in Egypt. God sent Moses and delivered them. Sadly, they began to make worthless idols that they used as their gods, similar to those they had left behind in Egypt and that had not saved them.

When people sleep at the wrong time, they end up doing the wrong things when they awake. Instead of thanking God and honoring him daily in gratitude, the Israelites soon forgot their misery in Egypt and began making idols to worship.

Sleeping at the wrong time can make us confused; this confusion leads to wayward ways that can jeopardize our current standing.

Instead of waiting and watching, Israel became busy doing the wrong things. God disapproved of their actions and punished them.

Our carelessness about sleep makes us inattentive. During the time when we are supposed to sleep, we do useless work; then, when the time to work comes, we want to sleep. Let us pray that God will deliver us from this state of confusion. Doing the right things at the wrong times will not yield the desired results because our actions are displaced.

When we sleep at the wrong time, people can steal the things that rightfully belong to us. By the time we discover this, it could be too late to repossess our possessions.

In the book of Genesis, the writer tells the story of Jacob and Esau; it is a story of treachery, greed, and dishonesty. Jacob and his mother connived and stole the blessing that was owed Esau because of his status as elder brother.

It was the second time Esau had lost to Jacob. The first time his birthright was stolen because of food; Esau carelessly gave away the one thing that authenticated his role as elder brother.

After returning from hunting, Esau rushed to bring delicious food to his father, Isaac, so that, as the elder son, he could receive Isaac's blessing.

However, instead of blessing Esau, his father Isaac said to him,

[17]Your brother came deceitfully and took your blessing. [Genesis 27:35]

The man of God, Job, knew how deceitful people can be. That is why he said,

[18]They conceive trouble and give birth to evil; their womb fashions deceit. [Job 15:35]

The mother loved Jacob more than she did Esau, even though she knew that, according to their customs, the elder brother inherited the blessings. She fought hard to manipulate the situation and to ensure that the blessing was given to the wrong person—Jacob, her beloved son.

For parents who love one child over others, this is a good lesson. We should love all our children equally and not divide them.

As I think about this story, I am left to wonder about a few things. Why would Jacob steal from Esau twice?

The first time was out of hunger, greed, and carelessness; Esau gave away his birthright to his younger brother Jacob for food. Because Esau had exchanged his birthright, his mother Rebecca and his brother sought to seal the deal by tricking Isaac into giving Jacob the real blessing that would solidify the birthright.

While Esau slept, his brother and mother tricked Isaac and stole the blessing, leaving him a servant to his younger brother.

Sleeping at the wrong time can cause you to lose things.

Nevertheless, there was a clause in the blessing contract that gave hope to Esau; it is a hope to all who, by carelessly sleeping, gave away the most precious things they had. This hope says that even though we messed up, there is still room for us at the cross.

This hope says that we qualify for the love, mercy, and grace of God regardless of our pasts. Whether we have lost our family, friends, jobs, or other opportunities, even if we have lost our own identities, there is still room to start over and make things better. There is hope. There is hope. There is hope!

As the story goes, Esau pleaded with his father Isaac to bless him too, with at least one blessing. In bitterness and tears, the old, blind Isaac said to his elder son, who should have taken the blessing of the firstborn that was stolen by his younger brother with the help of their mother,

¹⁹You will live by the sword and you will serve your brother. But when you grow restless, you will throw his yoke from off your neck. [Genesis 27:40]

The last sentence says that when Esau grows restless, he will break the yoke of servanthood to his younger brother and take his proper place as the elder brother with every right and privilege that entailed.

This is good news for all of us who have lost our proper places because of our failures. There is redemption in our seriousness. When we come to our senses and begin to take consistent, appropriate actions that create eligibility for eldership, God, by his divine grace, will forgive us and restore us.

God will restore us to leadership. We will not be at the mercy of others and wait in lines for rations; we will not be begging for leftovers. We will become the head and not the tail.

This is good news, but we must carefully examine the condition of the clause of hope in the contract of the blessings. This clause of hope is activated only by consistent, appropriate actions that warrant our eligibility to eldership. What does this mean? Carelessness caused us to lose our position in life and in God, so we must work hard to earn back that position. It won't come back if we do nothing. We must work hard to build those broken relationships.

We must rid ourselves of addictive substances that destroy our bodies. We must put aside bad habits, as well as bad friends who negatively influence us. We must stop going to bad places that promote our failures, and we must not corrupt good places by giving into our lust and evil gratifications.

Only when we demonstrate our ability to lead will God change things and give us our proper place in life. I long for this every day. May God help us.

Sleeping at the wrong time can make us ignore things we should do and make us do things we should not do at all.

When we sleep, our minds are dormant; some people sleepwalk and do weird things that normal people do not do. They do crazy things that they don't remember when they wake up. Please do not sleepwalk and act crazy.

There are people who married the wrong man or woman, who got into the wrong type of business, or who moved to the wrong place because they were sleepwalking. Now, their lives are messed up. They are so entangled in the situation and cannot find their way out. When we sleepwalk for a long time, we can become something we did not intend to be. Let us be very mindful about this. It is sad. It is bad.

When we sleep at the wrong time, we can find ourselves sitting with deceitful people; something that is not good at all.

This is what the psalmist said,

[20]*I do not sit with the deceitful, nor do I associate with hypocrites.* [Psalm 26:4]

Something terrible happens when we are not actively doing good things; anything can get us, anybody can lead us.

We should do good things and not let others deceive us. We should not associate with people who prey on others and drag them down the path of destruction.

Sometimes we are given opportunities to help others get out of certain unpleasant situations, but when we sleep, we will not even know the times.

There are times when people ask for assistance, and not always with their finances. These people need someone to affirm them, defend them, listen to them, console them, and encourage them; they just need affection.

When we open ourselves to help others, the Lord will remember us in our times of need. We can do this only when we are awake. Listen to this great story about helping a man in need,

²¹When Jesus reached the spot, he looked up and said to him, "Zacchaeus, come down immediately. I must stay at your house today." So he came down at once and welcomed him gladly. All the people saw this and began to mutter, "He has gone to be the guest of a sinner." [Luke 19:5-7]

The people refused the man Zacchaeus as a friend because of his history; people did not like him because of his work. Interestingly, Jesus became his friend, leading to Zacchaeus's restoration and new life. We can be there for others when they need us. We can be dependable.

When we sleep at the wrong time, we can become stagnant and complacency becomes our companion.

I think nobody in their right mind gets up in the morning and says, "Today I want to become wayward; today I want to become complacent." Waywardness and complacency come gradually when we put off things we should do and procrastinate; as time passes, it becomes a habit.

We become inconsistent, untrustworthy, and lazy; therefore, we become wayward and complacent. That is why King Solomon said that,

²²For the waywardness of the simple will kill them, and the complacency of fools will destroy them. [Proverbs 1:32]

Why must we become wayward and complacent when there is a lot to do? Why, when we are called to leadership, do we become simple instead of great? It is because we sleep; we sleep too much or at the wrong time.

When we are not active at a time we should be, we make room for evil. When we do not perform, or when we perform poorly at a time we should be achieving victory and making a name for ourselves, we dishonor ourselves and all the people connected to us.

We are not islands; we are a forest connected by shrubs, undergrowth, greens, swamps, creeks, ravines, rivers, and mangroves. We are not alone. That is why we must carefully consider our inactivity or activity before we commit ourselves to anything; there are consequences and real people are affected.

I want to challenge all of us to not sleep when we should be doing good things. The farmer who knew he had an enemy did nothing to protect his farm. His enemy took advantage of his weakness and sowed bad seeds. What have you lost as you slept?

Esau, sleeping while he was awake, sold his birthright to his younger brother Jacob for food. This led Jacob and his mother to steal the blessing of eldership.

Today many people sleep and play dead in the midst of important issues. People sleep and play dead in the midst of society's injustices, about which they can do something. That is not good at all.

I pray that all of us will hear the voice of God and take on our proper roles as leaders. I pray that we will not sleep when we are called upon to be leaders and champions.

If you were sleeping, wake up; it is time to work. If you were playing dead, wake up because you are not dead; start doing something meaningful with your life. The world is like a grand stage that needs performers. The arena is set. The audience is ready. They applaud top competitors, boo poor performers, and stone non-performers. Arise from your sleep. It is time to work.

Are you ready to perform when it is your time, or will you be sleeping or sleepwalking? The stage is set. The audience is waiting—do something!

Chapter 4: Obedience Brings Victory

Obedience calls for respect, agreement, conformity, and honor. To obey someone is to submit to their leadership. We obey people and people obey us. When we do this, we can live and work together in spite of our differences.

We will not agree at all times. We do not believe the same things everyone else does. Our cultures, norms, and values may be different. This is perfectly okay because diversity is a compliment.

To obey or be obeyed, we do not have to agree about everything. Mutual respect and understanding involves valuing the interests of others.

People prefer simple obedience to anything we can do as a substitute. When we obey someone, we say to them that we respect their opinion and are willing to carry it out. We submit because others submit to us. Obedience must be reciprocal, not necessarily to the same person, but to others.

Everyday friends obey each other. Kids obey their parents and parents honor their kids. Teammates obey each other, and must definitely obey their coaches in the same manner that employees must obey their supervisors and managers. When we obey each other in this manner, mutual understanding leads to mutual benefits. We create a "win-win" situation.

Obedience is so important that Prophet Samuel reminded King Saul about how God regarded it, especially at a time when the king never followed orders but instead took matters into his own hands to please his soldiers.

Prophet Samuel spoke to King Saul and asked,

[23]Does the Lord has great delight in burnt offerings and sacrifices, as much as in obeying the Lord? To obey is better than sacrifice, and to heed than the fat of rams. [I Samuel 15:22]

One critical lesson to learn from King Saul and Prophet Samuel is that we must follow orders, especially during critical times. Mistakes are not tolerated. Any disobedience will incur consequences, some of them severe.

In our world today, many people act like King Saul, overlooking simple instructions and doing things contrary to them. Instead of following simple orders, people do their own things. When the time comes for accountability, they provide a number of invalid excuses.

Prophet Samuel made it very clear to King Saul that no sacrifice can substitute for simple obedience. It is better to listen and obey than to do other things as though they were more important than the instructions given.

It is sad that we are all, in some way, guilty of this. We do not like to do things that are inconvenient. We like to do things our way and in our time. We agree to put in extra time and energy and prepare fixed answers when people ask us. This is not good at all.

I have seen students who blamed teachers when they, the students, failed exams. Even though the teachers provided notes, lectures, and assignments, the students did not study, so they failed.

When this happens, instead of correcting their mistakes and working hard, they see the teachers as the problem. The students' deniability and arrogance are so sickening.

Many Christians complain to God every day because life is difficult. They are poor, sick, and broke. Many of us must check ourselves before we blame God and innocent people for our own failures. It is not fair to blame others for something that we can control.

The Bible says that,

[24]His divine power has granted to us all things that pertain to life and godliness, through the knowledge of him who called us to his own glory and excellence. [II Peter 1:3]

I am left to wonder: Why do we not know the power, see it working for us, so that we can have life and enjoy godliness because of our knowledge of God? This reminds me of what Prophet Samuel said to King Saul about obedience and sacrifice.

It seems as though many people work overtime to make sacrifices and excuses instead of simply obeying the Word. Whenever we do this, we limit the power of God in our lives, and his glory does not manifest in us.

When we do not obey God's commands and when we do not say yes to love, righteous living, worship, church attendance, tithes and offerings, evangelism, and charity, we do not reap the benefits of obedience. We must remember that obedience—not vain sacrifices and cheap worship—brings blessings.

Chapter 4:1 - Obey and Learn

It is very important for all followers to obey and learn. If we want to become leaders, we must first learn to obey.

Good followers make good leaders. Bad followers produce tyrants.

The overwhelming significance of obeying and learning led God to give special instructions to Joshua.

^{25}But be very careful to keep the commandment and the law that Moses the servant of the LORD gave you: to love the LORD your God, to walk in obedience to him, to keep his commands, to hold fast to him and to serve him with all your heart and with all your soul. [Joshua 22:5]

Joshua was told to obey and learn. This sort of obedience involves not just the intellect and experience, but also the keeping of commands with one's whole heart and soul. Just like Joshua, we are required to learn and obey because there is no other way to be found in the Lord than to trust him, obey him, and learn from him.

Many Christians today do not grow in the Lord because they do not want to obey and learn. They want God to solve all their problems before they obey him, yet they pray every day for God to bless them.

There are many people who do not want to obey and learn from their teachers, mentors, bosses, pastors, and parents. They neglect the fact that when we learn from these teachers in life, we understand the subject matter and many times perform better than our teachers do.

Instead of simply being humble and allowing another person to pour knowledge into them, they wander aimlessly out of arrogance and ignorance. They put on big shows with nothing to back their claims, and all because they did not let someone teach them.

We should never consider as wasted the time we take to be humble, obey, and learn. No, not at all. As a matter of fact, one day, when we look back, we will be glad we achieved our education. Those of us who are grateful will appreciate the people who taught us.

Chapter 4:2 - Know What You Learn

As good as it is to obey, the process benefits nothing if we do not actually know what we have learned. Joshua was told,

26But take diligent heed to do the commandment and the law, which Moses the servant of the LORD charged you, to love the LORD your God, and walk in all his ways, and to keep his commandments, and to cleave unto him, and to serve him with all your heart and with all your soul. [Joshua 22:5]

To hold fast and serve means knowing him to a degree at which we can apply the knowledge carefully. We must all follow Joshua's lead and understand what we learn; otherwise, we will not be able to use our knowledge.

The blessings of God come only through obedience to the Word. It is when we do what the Word says that we experience the bountiful blessings found in the word of God.

To benefit from knowledge, we must apply it. Intellectual knowledge is not sufficient, as it may not lead us to action. Experiential knowledge is good, as it gives us a first-hand encounter. However, the combination of both is far better.

The Prophet Zechariah had this to say,

27This is what the LORD Almighty says: "If you will walk in obedience to me and keep my requirements, then you will govern my house and have charge of my courts, and I will give you a place among these standing here." [Zechariah 3:7]

To walk in obedience, we must follow certain requirements, some of which are as simple as knowing what we learned. Our time in the classroom of life will be wasted if we do not know what we've been taught. When we do not know what we learn, we waste precious time and resources.

Without proper application, knowledge becomes an experience that we will soon forget. The combination of intellectual and experiential knowledge—and its proper application—provides a great benefit to whoever pursues it. This is why we must obey and learn, but we must also ensure that we really know what we learn.

CHAPTER 4:3 - APPLY WHAT YOU KNOW

Many people go around doing nothing when they have something good to offer society. They possess certain talents, gifts, and abilities that would take them forward and be a blessing to others. To everybody's loss, they refuse to take the stage and show what they know. This is not good at all.

Jesus said that we should not light a lamp and cover it when it is supposed to give light for people to see in the dark.

[28]No one lights a lamp, then hides it in a drawer. It's put on a lamp stand so those entering the room have light to see where they're going. [Luke 11:33]

John, the gospel writer, said this about love and obedience,

[29]And this is love: that we walk in obedience to his commands. As you have heard from the beginning, his command is that you walk in love. [II John 1:6]

We must walk in obedience to the commands of God and do what they say. There is a certain joy to be had when we apply the knowledge we have acquired and when things work as we have been taught they should. It is quite exhilarating.

We experience joy when we do what we know; our teachers in life have expressed joy in seeing us do what they have taught us. We must keep something in mind, though; our teachers expect us to build on what we know and develop it.

Chapter 4:4 - Build on What You Know

The Apostle Paul told young Timothy,

[30]For this reason I am reminding you to fan into flame the gift of God, which is in you through the laying on of my hands. [II Timothy 1:6]

Once we have obeyed and learned, and once we know what we have learned and have begun to apply it, we must build on our acquired knowledge. We cannot simply proceed with the old things we have learned when the world is advancing every day.

Jesus said that we cannot put new wine into old wineskins.

[31]Neither do people pour new wine into old wineskins. If they do, the skins will burst; the wine will run out and the wineskins will be ruined. No, they pour new wine into new wineskins, and both are preserved. [Matthew 9:17]

New knowledge cannot be applied to old systems. Some things—like ideologies, technologies, systems, and even places—need to change as new knowledge emerges. We should apply imagination and the power of creativity to find new ways of doing things and to build on them.

Chapter 4:5 - Excel and Be Innovative

Excellence and innovation go hand in hand. Once we begin to build on what we learn, letting it flow in becomes easy. When we build on what we have learned, we must be creative and innovative. We can find other ways to get things done.

The Bible teaches us to,

[32] Walk in obedience to all that the LORD your God has commanded you, so that you may live and prosper and prolong your days in the land that you will possess. [Deuteronomy 5:33]

To live long and prosper in the land is good for all of us. When we begin to innovate and pursue excellence, our work or ministry brings us joy. When we have joy, we prosper and live in peace; we enjoy a long life.

Obedience is so important to the attainment of prosperity and longevity. Creativity is necessary in our daily operations. Life becomes interesting when we have something to live for, something good and meaningful.

We must excel and be innovative. We must not hold new ideas in old containers.

The desire to excel and be innovative propels us in a certain direction to move forward.

This brings us to the next stage. As I said earlier, we must obey and learn, know what we learn, apply what we know, build on what we know, and excel and be innovative; all this is good. But after we have achieved this, we must go beyond what we have learned. If we do not want our visions to die, we must go a step further.

Chapter 4:6 - Outgrow What You Learned

As we excel and innovate, something wonderful happens—we outgrow what we learned in the beginning.

God expects us to outgrow what we learned yesterday and to build something new today. He expects us to be so innovative that we outgrow what we have today and focus on the future. Our parents expect us to go beyond what they have done and to do better. Our teachers believe that we will someday learn more than what they have taught us.

Simply living on knowledge from others—without adding our own method, style, and signature to it—does a disservice to our teachers. As we grow and as technology improves, we can do better. We must create a signature series.

The Apostle Paul, in talking to the church in Corinth about overcoming evil powers, said,

[33] And we will be ready to punish every act of disobedience, once your obedience is complete. [II Corinthians 10:6]

While this refers to overcoming evil, I want to dig into it for our current topic. This passage says that, when our own obedience is complete, we can punish and discipline others for their acts of disobedience. When we have completed our learning, we can be in charge. When we are in charge, we can create our signature series, a special mode of doing things by which everyone recognizes us. Everybody will know that it was you who did something because of the special touch you add to it—something nice that only you like to do.

Chapter 4:7 - Create Your Signature Series

God has given us diversity. All of us have our own ways of doing things. We all have different things we like. When we outgrow what we learn, we do not necessarily limit our ideologies based on what we have learned; instead, we take things a step further.

When we know what we have learned and that we have outgrown it, we are left with only two options: to create something new by building on existing things, or to create something entirely new altogether.

We can touch and tweak old things and give them a whole new look. This way of doing and presenting things is known as our signature.

If you have not created a signature series, you are living someone else's dreams and living in their brain. If you have not created your signatures, you have not offered anything to the world. You are using only what was given, and living this way will soon make you bored.

God said to the children of Israel,

[34]If you fully obey the Lord your God and carefully follow all his commands I give you today, the Lord your God will set you high above all the nations on earth. [Deuteronomy 28:1]

What is this about? God says that if we carefully follow his commands, he will lift us high above the nations of the earth. People who are above must do things like those previously mentioned; they create law and order. They have enough to share. The only way we can achieve this is to use our brains, create a signature series, and apply our minds.

Chapter 5: Apply Your Mind

We thank God for the great minds he has given humanity. It is so good to be in a place that has a number of great minds, as well as smart and intelligent people. They make life easy for everyone.

Inasmuch as we share our gratitude for the blessing of having smart people in the world, we must learn to use our own minds, too. Whether your head is big or small, you have brains in it. We must use our brains like the other great minds out there and make some contribution to society.

Many people like to put their current situations above their capabilities. Yes, it is true that many of us have reasons to fold our legs, clasp our hands, and cry and complain about how life is bad; we can do that. We can even criticize the government and say that it is not serving the people correctly. We can criticize our favorite sports team for the fact that it lost a game, and we can even complain about how bad the weather is. However, all this profits nothing.

Some people blame life on the place where they live; they see nothing except bad things. Instead of digging in like others to make something happen, they sit back and do nothing except complain, and complain, and complain.

In contrast to all this, I have learned that the Bible teaches,

[35]All things God works for the good of those who love him, who have been called according to his purpose." [Romans 8:28]

Instead of whining and crying about how bad life is, we must understand that God works all things out for the good of those called by his name. As the children of God, we must see that our experiences—even the bad ones—can be turned around for good.

While we may not entirely understand how God works with the bad things in life to achieve good, we must trust that the Lord knows how to take care of us. For those who question whether God works all things in our favor, let me say this to you.

Many of us are not medical doctors and surgeons who care for the sick, but we trust them to do their jobs correctly. In the same manner, since we are not God—not omniscient, omnipotent, and almighty—we must let God be God and not worry about every process he uses to work out all things for our good. All we have to do is work on our part of the equation.

The Apostle Paul, speaking to the church in Rome, said,

[36]*Do not be conformed any longer to the pattern of this world, but be transformed by the renewing of your mind. Then you will be able to test and approve what God's will is – his good, pleasing, and perfect will.* [Romans 12:2]

He talks about different patterns, ways, designs, structures, and forms we are not to follow when applying our minds. We must learn to leave behind old patterns and let the transformation of our minds occur; we need renewed minds.

Jesus said that we cannot put new wine in old wineskins; in the same manner, we cannot keep an old mind while desiring to do new things. It does not work like that. With a renewed mind, we can test things to ensure that they line up correctly with the word of God and with our times.

When we apply our minds, we please God, country, group, family, and self.

Dull, inactive, wasteful minds are a liability and threat to society. They become troublemakers over time.

A neighborhood full of stupid people never advances; the same is true for families that lack good minds. We must not waste good brains; instead, we must work our minds.

[37]*And do this, understanding the present time. The hour has come for you to wake up from your slumber, because our salvation is nearer now than we first believed.* [Romans 11:13]

We are commanded to do something—to understand the present time. We must understand that we are no longer in the 1800s, nor the

1950s, so we should not act like we are. Knowledge acquired during those years has since been improved upon.

We are not riding horses anymore; we use cars with muscle and lots of electronics. We have computer phones and we fly planes and we are now trying to move to Mars and other places.

Everyone who is sleeping must wake up because good things are closer than we think. If you do not wake up in time, the good stuff will pass over you. You will be left behind while your friends and family advance.

Apply your mind and understand the times; things are changing every day. Wake up from your wayward ways and start preparing yourself for the challenges and blessings at hand. If you must go to school, please do so. If you must change your business, just do it.

Some people must move away from their neighborhoods, as they have certain associations that are not good for them. It is not that prayer cannot answer anything, but when the answer to your prayer is a suggestion that you move, you must obey the voice of God and do so. Stop fighting unnecessary, never-ending battles.

If you are in business, spy on your own workplace and see it through a client's eyes. You will be surprised to discover the reasons why things are not going well. Maybe your products and services must be updated, or your customer service needs improvement. Do not simply sit back; instead, do something proactive to make things better. Use your brains; I believe you have some.

It is interesting what the Apostle Paul said to the church at Ephesus,

[38]Be very careful, then, how you live – not as unwise but as wise, making the most of every opportunity, because the days are evil. Therefore, do not be foolish, but understand what the Lord's will is. [Ephesians 5:15]

The Apostle Paul admonished the believers to be careful about how they lived their lives. I say, be careful about how you work, go to school, do business, raise your kids, and deal with your spouse. You must act like a wise—not a foolish—person.

Make the most of every opportunity.

Good things do not come knocking over and over again always. We must seize the opportunities we get in life.

I want you to think about the founder of Microsoft, Bill Gates; the founder of Facebook, Mark Zuckerberg; the founder of Dell Inc., Michael Dell; and the founder of Apple and the iPhone, Steve Jobs. All of these guys saw opportunities and seized them. How about you and me? Should we sit back and complain about the government, world markets, sunshine, and rainfalls instead of doing something better?

Today the world knows these men. They make billions and we all love them because they contributed something positive to life. They make life better for us.

Now what about you and me? These days are evil. We cannot be foolish and simply sit around doing nothing except sleeping, eating, gambling, playing cards, chasing after women and men aimlessly, partying, drinking, smoking, or getting high.

Others are using their heads, working their brains, and applying their minds. What about you? When was the last time you really looked at the puzzle of your own life and tried to solve it?

I know some people are ready to blame everything on society, the government, corruption, and everything else, but I will tell you something that will surprise you.

In the same place where you are complaining, whining, and crying (in other words, doing nothing), people like you are fighting hard every day to make things happen. Surprisingly, they are doing well. They have learned to prosper during a recession and bad times.

They know the government might be negligent in some areas, and that their families may not care about their wellbeing so much. However, for them, sitting down, crying, and doing nothing are not options. They have resolved to get up, go out there, and struggle hard until they find something to hang on. They do not mind trying many things that don't work; instead, they never stop trying.

I know plenty of us have reasons to sit back and complain about life, the government, the economy, our families, and similar things. Your complaints may be legitimate, but they do not put food on your table. It is hard work, but if you refuse to give up in the midst of fierce odds, you will have food, a place to rest your head, and money in your pocket.

Let me be frank with you. Just like you, I have several problems involving family, school, church, mission, personal projects, and the like.

Life can be hard; I know. I had things. I had people. However, I lost many precious people and things. I worked and used my money to help others; I even helped some people pay their rent.

I did a lot of charity work, but when the time came, the very people for whom I was running up and down betrayed me, abandoned me, and began to seek my downfall. Life can be tough; I know.

In the middle of the night, I will get up to take people to work or to pick up someone from work who missed the bus. I used to take to work people who were assigned to places that offered no public transportation. I worked hard to help others.

But all these people for whom I sacrificed left me, insulted me, and did not even greet me anymore when they saw me. I know what backstabbing is; I am so familiar with betrayal, neglect, and abandonment.

I know what it means to be broke. I also know what it means to be so broke that no one wants to help, even the people I lavished my money and time on in the past. I know it hurts. It really hurts.

I had every reason to stay in bed and cry. I had every reason to hate people. To tell the truth, if I had had my way, I would have rather shot some people dead because of how hurt I was! The hurt began to eat me up slowly. To make things worse, I had people blaming me, saying that I was the cause of my own trouble.

But when I looked at all these things, I remembered my philosophy in life:

"With God above all things, life is but what one makes it."

I paused for a moment and said this to myself over and over and over again until the words sank into my ears. Then they sank deep into my heart and spirit. I knew that I should not stay bitter and blame life's problems on tragedies.

I knew that I should not let negativity consume my life. I knew that I had to find a way to switch from negative thoughts to positive thoughts.

I got in my vehicle and drove around Phoenix from Northern Avenue to the I-17 Freeway southbound; from the I-10 eastbound to the 202 northbound to the 101 eastbound until I got back on the I-10 westbound and exited on 35th Avenue straight to the church for a time of prayer. I was there alone with no other church members or family members.

I was there without the prayer team. There were no choirs and no deacons; there was no pianist—I was alone. In the emptiness of the sanctuary, I sought the face of God desperately. I wanted to hear God.

Sometimes when the road gets tough, it is okay to get some *"me time"* separate from others and to seek the face of God alone. I prayed so hard and cried unto the Lord to remedy my pain.

I prayed until I was out of words; I revealed my soul before the Lord. As I was lying prostrate before the Lord, I felt a cool feeling come over me. Nothing was said, but somehow it gave me assurance that things would be okay.

I stayed there for a moment to enjoy the presence of the Lord in quietude. I was swallowed up in deep peace and tranquility. For that moment I could not see, think, or feel my problems. The weight was lifted off me. I began to feel this unexplainable bliss of joy come over me. I was just happy without cause; I was full of joy. I rose, lifted my hands, and began to worship.

Sometimes we need some *"me time"* to search ourselves and to spend some time before the Lord. I was at a place where nothing mattered to me. Nothing could bring me joy and happiness; I was so sorrowful, yet I kept this to myself.

I had only one friend I could trust with my personal issues; I trusted him so much that I did not need to grease my talks around him. We talked to each other as men, and as men of God.

Somewhere in the middle of this mess, even my friend became angry about some things and did not want to talk to me. Oh, how I wish I had the chance to speak to him about everything and pray. I needed his company desperately, but I did not get that. The problems were separating me from people I loved so much; I was alone.

The ones who hurt me went about their business as though nothing was wrong. They went to church and did all the "church stuff." It appeared that God somehow approved of their actions while I was in tears. They seemed to be blessed while I suffered in the anguish of my soul. This was ridiculous.

I agree with Job because sometimes it seems as though evildoers go free and avoid facing the Lord's justice while the righteous suffer.

³⁹The groans of the dying rise from the city, and the souls of the wounded cry out for help. But the Lord charges no one with wrongdoing." [Job 24:12]

The good and the innocent suffer at the hands of wicked people, and the Lord does nothing. I know that feeling. It is quite terrible.

People who never knew the letter "A" from bullfrog—people whom I had helped—spoke bad things about me to my face after gossiping about me from house to house. Some pastors from my country despised me as though I were a pedophile or serial killer.

Yet despite all the ingratitude, slander, and affronts, I never gave in to the desire for retaliation. I know deep down in my heart that the God of love is also the God of justice. I know that my redeemer lives.

⁴⁰I know that my redeemer lives, and that in the end he will stand on the earth. [Job 19:25]

I know that God will justify me. I know that God will see me through. Those who sought to break me down so that they could elevate their own positions will have God to contend with. I will overcome; I will overcome everything.

I know that weeping may endure for a night, but that joy comes in the morning.

⁴¹Weeping may stay for a night, but rejoicing comes in the morning. [Psalm 3:5]

I know that this dark night of the soul will pass. I know nothing lasts forever; even bad people have to sleep.

Regardless of how bad my life may be, I do not give in; I do not give up. People tried to put me on edge so that I would say or do something I would regret, but the Lord helped me keep my silence.

I want you to know that sometimes when people push you, you must remain quiet and wait on the Lord. He can settle the matter better than you can. Regardless of your circumstance, trust God and use your head.

Why did I tell you this thing about myself? I want you to know that God understands our humanity, yet works with us in spite of the situation. I have to tell you that in our time of trouble and suffering, we can put forth the powers of creativity, bravery, and determination. You can apply your mind in good times and in bad.

As a matter of fact, many times our best ideas come to us when things are rough; challenges seem to bring out the best in us. Oh, come on my friend, I know you can do better in hard times and in good times. I challenge you today to use your head. Apply your mind. The world is looking for people like you.

PART THREE:
DROP THE STUFF!

There are unnecessary loads we carry around that make life more difficult than it needs to be. It does not have to be this way. We must let go of certain things, places, and people that bring us nothing but harm.

You will discover that some of the people you must let go of are your friends and family, but this is okay. Sometimes we must tarry alone, reflect, adjust, and move on.

If your friends or family were actually true to you, they would never become an enemy of your progress. Any time one of them falls into this category, you must treat him or her as such until the situation returns to normal.

Do not let those who are supposed to lift you up become the ones to kill you slowly. There are traitors everywhere. Beware!

Drop the Stuff!

- Stinking Thinking
- Stupid Friends
- Bad Places
- Extra Load

Chapter 6: Stinking Thinking

There is a lot about the way we think that affects our lives. Every day, every hour, every minute, and every second our minds are preoccupied with different thoughts jamming through them.

The things we think about become the things we do. Even if others tell us some things that would put us into action, we must develop the will to either do them or not do them. I say this because every day we employ our minds to think, consider, delve, examine, and explore things—to do or not do them in their time and sequence.

In our world today, learning institutions across the globe teach the mind how to think so that it yields good results. These schools help mold us into the beings we are, with myriad professions and skills to contribute to society.

We learn things and think about things that make an impact, whether significant or insignificant. This makes me remember a proverb that says,

[42]As a man thinks in his heart, so is he. [Proverbs 23:7]

In simple words, the way we think is the way we are. It is disconcerting to believe that we can live our lives doing things totally different from the way we think. That would be very difficult, if not impossible.

Do not get me wrong. Some people live in duplicity without remorse for a season. For example, those in the intelligence field must "be like the bad guys" to catch the bad guys. I also know that movie stars must act out their characters. However, even these people must think to fulfill their roles; thinking is that important.

I know about criminal profiling and intelligence gathering. These people act out their lives in a way that helps catch culprits for homeland security or other special interests. Even so, they must do double the thinking that most of us do; to perform such tasks, they must put their minds to work and think harder than the average person, beyond their own boundaries and comfort zones.

We make computers, robots, and other machinery with membranes that enable them to perform certain functions routinely. Because of this, automated machines make production easier and help the marketplace operate more efficiently.

This leads me to wonder: If man-made things like computers, cranes, robots, and other machinery can "think" and "remember," what about us humans? To what degree are we supposed to think? How much are we supposed to use our brains?

I once heard that a human generally uses less than thirty percent of his or her brain power in a lifetime. If it is true that we become what we think, I think thinking is a very serious matter. We must really begin to put our brains to work.

Looking back at your life, are you proud of the way you thought about things that got you where you are today? This is something serious to consider. Our thoughts have a great impact.

Are you one of those people whose lives are filled with regrets because of things you have done or things you did not do? Are you among the happy campers whose thoughts and deeds have landed them where they are today and are lifting them higher and higher? Where did your thoughts take you? Did your thoughts take you up or down? Now I think you are beginning to understand the importance of the way we think. It can build us or break us. Beware my friend; the things you think can affect you.

In a letter to the church in Rome, the Apostle Paul wrote something from which we can all benefit:

^{43}Therefore, I urge you, brothers and sisters, in view of God's mercy, to offer your bodies as a living sacrifice, holy and pleasing to God – this is your true and proper worship. ^{2} Do not conform to the pattern of this world, but be transformed by the renewing of your mind. Then you will be able to test and approve what God's will is – his good, pleasing and perfect will. [Romans 12:1-2]

Though this was written to the early Christians, it has some unique aspects that inform our discussion on thinking. Proper thinking does not discriminate in terms of class, religion, ethnicity, culture, or age; it concerns all of us.

The Apostle Paul made a clear point that true worshippers must offer their bodies as living sacrifices to God. The second part says that worshippers should not be conformed to the pattern of this world, but should instead be transformed by the renewing of the mind.

True worshippers' minds must be renewed so that their thoughts and ways of life—including their bodies—can be offered to the honor of God. The mind should control the body; the body should not lead the mind.

I must admit, though, that there is a level of maturity we can reach whereby our hearts and minds work in unison to achieve a better state of existence. If the two can work together, it will be hard for us to go wrong.

Why? Because we will think carefully about anything and exhaust every possible alternative before making a decision. However, if, after we have collected all the data, things are still not clear-cut, we must employ our hearts or gut feelings to lead our minds to proper action.

When we are at this level, we think before we talk; as a matter of fact, we listen more and talk less. We think carefully about the implications and consequences of our actions before we do certain things. It saves us from unnecessary trouble.

Before we reach that point, we must let our minds properly lead us, even if our feelings and emotions want to take us somewhere else. We must work on it.

Everywhere, peoples' minds must be renewed so that they entertain new thoughts and are both adaptable and innovative. Some people want to use old ideas when there are new and better ways to do things. The use of old ideas in our modern world looks eccentric and ridiculous; old ideologies must be retired or improved upon for today's world.

Today people make fast luxury vehicles and planes; who wants to ride a horse or elephant, or have people carry them in a hammock from one city to another? Imagine living in hot places like Arizona in the summer, or in tropical terrains like Liberia during the rainy season. Wouldn't that be absurd, considering the advances made in transportation?

Interestingly, some people want to live in "yesterday" and think like people from yesterday when we are making great advances today and planning for a better tomorrow. Some people's best ideas are obsolete.

These ideas have expired before we can even use them; what they have to say is history. However, please do not think that all old ideas do not apply today; instead, we need to think new and think straight.

Stinking Thinking has terrible effects. When people have Stinking Thinking, they do not do anything to improve themselves. They become lazy and blame other people for their misery.

Leaders with Stinking Thinking take part in corruption and the mismanagement of national resources. Development is difficult, if not impossible.

Pastors and church leaders with Stinking Thinking prey on people. They take advantage of people's weakness and benevolence and relieve them of their cash. They use women and men for their ungodly pleasures. Basically, pastors like that take advantage of God's people.

When you have a Stinking Thinking wife, you are finished; while you are building your future, she goes around gossiping and spending family money on useless things.

A husband with Stinking Thinking does not love his wife and children. Instead, he goes about womanizing and bringing into the world more kids when he cannot support the ones he has at home. He sometimes brings home sexually transmitted diseases to his faithful wife.

He takes much-needed family cash to gamble and comes home with empty hands; he may become lazy and sit back as though there is no life in him.

When poor people have Stinking Thinking, they cheat and kill each other as the rich plunder their land and take natural resources for pennies on the dollar. Stinking Thinking leaders take bribes and rob their countries of things that truly belong to the people.

They hail the rich as gods and command citizens to stand in line to salute them. The people who steal are the people the victims take to be friends. I guess they are partners in crime.

What more can I say to convince you that Stinking Thinking is a self-inflicting disease that must be healed? People must be delivered from it. It is a curse that must be broken for us to have freedom and live like normal people.

Stinking Thinking fosters family feuds. It destroys businesses. It incites wars. Stinking Thinking brought about slavery. It sparks discrimination and injustice, and slows national progress. It was Stinking Thinking that led Hitler to kill six million Jews during the Holocaust.

Stinking Thinking makes African leaders think that, in their countries, presidency is a family business. After they are elected (or after they have coerced their way to election), they would rather die in power than give way to democracy.

Every year, many people commit suicide because they feel as though they have no way to live; this, despite the fact that thousands of benevolent people and organizations are there to help them in their plight.

This is because Stinking Thinking tells them that there is no hope and that the best thing to do is to kill themselves. When you have Stinking Thinking, your life does not go forward.

It can make you jealous of people who are ahead of you. Instead of befriending them so that they can teach you how they made it, you fill your mind with evil plots to bring them down.

There is nothing good about Stinking Thinking. All there is, and all there has been, is trouble for humanity. Moses, the author of the Pentateuch, wrote,

⁴⁴The Lord saw how great the wickedness of the human race had become on the earth, and that every inclination of the thoughts of the human heart was only evil all the time. [Genesis 6:4-6]

There are some people who do not seem to think about anything good. All their thoughts and ways are evil. Let me ask you—what are your thoughts? Are they evil or good? If your thoughts are evil, please reconsider them and change.

There is something good about you that you must give to society—the world needs your ideas.

It can be frustrating for us as parents to see our children doing stupid and evil things while their friends are improving their own lives. We may be good, but our children are so different, as though they were not our own blood. They seem to come from hell because they are so stupid and wicked. It makes us regret that they were even born.

Whether it is a parent crying out in frustration, or a country crying out about the evil thoughts and wickedness of its people, the truth remains that Stinking Thinking fosters myriad evils unimaginable to humankind.

It is a sad truth that God knows what we think, but gives us the freedom and the will to channel our lives. It is written that,

[45]The Lord knows the thoughts of man, that they are vanity. [Psalm 94:11]

We do not have to live with vain, empty and useless thoughts; we can do better than that. Some people are not wicked; they are just negative. They see everything in the wrong way; they have crazy and weird explanation for things.

They think that everyone hates them and that the world is coming for them. The truth is that nothing of the sort is going on; it is only in their heads and is not real. They would be free of the useless weights they carry if only they could think in a positive manner.

Maybe you have someone like that in your life. Negative people are difficult to deal with; they are just hard to have around.

Not everyone who entertains Stinking Thinking enjoys it; their troubles simply have a way of putting them in a terrible state of mind. It's like what Job said,

[46]My troubled thoughts prompt me to answer because I am greatly disturbed. [Job 20:2]

And as King David, king of Israel, said,

[47]My thoughts trouble me and I am distraught. [Psalm 55:2]

Let me ask you: how well do you think when life has brought pressure upon you? Do you let the troubles of life get the best of you, and even turn you into something you are not?

When such things occur, we can give in to them or we can stand our ground. We can keep our integrity because we cannot allow the misfortunes of life to change our thinking or our character. We are better than that!

Occasionally, we all think like the wicked. King David once said,

[48] *In his pride the wicked man does not seek him; in all his thoughts there is no room for God.* [Psalm 10:4]

It is interesting to note that today some people think there is no God. Some rich people think there is no God because their money can pay for almost everything.

They think that it is only the needy who need God—those who cry out to any deity for help. Some intellectuals think that there is no God; in vain, they explain the "God factor" using empty words of philosophy to fill empty heads.

While the rich spitefully think that it is the poor and needy who need God because of what they lack, not all poor people are fond of God. Some believe that there is no God because they do not see him or feel his love and care.

When the troubles of life come at us, we find it easy to wonder if God really exists, much less cares about us. In the midst of riches, knowledge, and power (and even in the midst of sickness, poverty, famine, wars, loneliness, and deprivation), it is easy to question the very existence of God and his character. However, I want you to know this,

The blatant denial or ignorance about a person, place or thing, does not in any way impeccably obliterate the existence and impact of that person, place, or thing, neither does it exonerate the adherent in any manner; the same is true of God.

Just because some rich, powerful, or intellectual person does not believe that God exists, we do not have to believe the same. This is true about the poor and needy as well. God is.

It is we who must try to find God; through discovery of him, we will know how much he wants to take us to higher heights. The writer of Hebrews wrote,

⁴⁹And without faith it is impossible to please God, because anyone who comes to him must believe that he exists and that he rewards those who earnestly seek him. [Hebrews 11:6]

There are some who do not know God. Could it be because they have not sought him, or because they are completely ignorant about him?

To believe a thing, we must first think about the possibility of its existence. When we prejudge the non-existence of God, we find it hard to open our hearts and minds to the possibility that God is.

Interestingly, to find God, we must begin to think that there is a God. Once we know that, we can take the next step—accepting the possibility of God's existence.

This sort of thought can help us carefully consider whether or not God exists. By thinking about it, we can disprove or approve the existence of God. When we accept that God is, we will discover that he rewards those who diligently seek him; but first we must believe that he is.

Stinking Thinking dulls our minds and incapacitates our will to think deeply; we become those who just accept things the way they are to our loss.

When we do this, we essentially pack our tools, turn our minds away from the gold fields, and run after everything that shines, thinking it is gold. We take things for granted without weighing them properly. Stinking Thinking is a terrible diseases that needs a cure. It is my prayer that God will help cure our Stinking Thinking.

When we take part in Stinking Thinking, we will end up with ugly behaviors because we are what we think. Some people would do better if they would simply snap out of the bad behaviors and stupid thoughts they have brought upon themselves.

To change, we must think differently, as it is our thoughts—or lack of them—that fuels our behavior. If you have anyone in your life like this, please pray for them. You might need to send them to a good counselor or provide them with good company so that they can see life in a new and better way. Stinking Thinking has destroyed and killed many people; please do not let this happen to you. If you are caught up in it, know that there is a solution. Do not spend another day of your short life this way. Drop the Stuff—Stinking Thinking.

Chapter 7: Stupid Friends

In life, it is crucial to truly know the people we consider our friends. Friends, like spouses, have a way of making or breaking us. They have the power to lead us to success or dump us into trouble.

We must be careful—very careful—of whom we make our friends. Sometimes it is better to have acquaintances than to call everyone we meet a friend. There is a difference between all the people we know and those who are our friends. It is better to have no friends at all than to have Stupid Friends.

Before you start going around and calling everyone who gets on your nerves a "Stupid Friend," let me help you understand the definition. Stupid Friends are dimwitted, brainless, unintelligent, thick-skulled, and empty-headed people.

Such people have nothing good to offer. If we are not careful, they can take away our very essence. I call all such friends "Stupid Friends" because of their character, the way they talk, and their manner of life.

There is a proverb that says,

[50]*Birds of the same feather flock together.*

In discussing Stupid Friends, we must consider who we bring close to us. We must consider who influences our thoughts and actions. The Bible teaches us that,

[51]*Blessed is the one who does not walk in step with the wicked or stand in the way that sinners take or sit in the company of mockers.* [Psalm 1:1]

When we do not walk in the steps of the wicked, or stand in the way of sinners, or sit in the company of mockers, we can become blessed in life. Being wicked to others is not a good thing; when we treat people in a wicked way, their first thought is payback.

When we associate with people with lots of moral defects, they rub on us and dull our minds toward insensitivity.

When we sit with those who mock people for their misfortunes and who laugh at their lack, we bring disgrace upon innocent souls; this is not good at all. Bad seeds have a way of growing; beware.

This is why the passage says that, when we do not do this, God will bless us. It is not a good thing to be friends with wicked people, morally defective people, and people who do nothing but evil. It is not a good thing at all.

The Apostle Paul wrote to the church in Corinth about Stupid Friends when he said,

[52]*Do not be misled: "Bad company corrupts good character."*
[I Corinthians 15:33]

Who brings bad company? Stupid Friends bring bad company; they are so stupid that they have nothing good to offer. There are people today who think that they can hang around with bad and foolish people and not be affected by their actions.

Some people do not smoke, but they are always in the company of people who smoke like chimneys and old, rusty car exhaust pipes. These people forget that secondhand smoke is as dangerous as actually smoking. They are getting sick without their knowledge. Stupid Friends can make you sick.

Some people regularly go to bars and nightclubs with Stupid Friends, but believe that they will remain morally sound; they do not believe that they will behave badly in any way. They believe that they will not smoke, drink, or have a quickie or one-night stand. Their minds mislead them into thinking that they can have fun and go home clean.

They forget that many things go on in these places—things that can corrupt a decent, moral person. The dangling chills and smoothness of alcohol, the cool music that sets the right mood, the luring guys and girls who are so inviting—in a place where anything goes, anything is possible.

Despite the fact that moral people may deny the impact of such bad company, it is only a manner of time before they join the fun and mess up their good lives. The newbie is the one who usually gets in trouble at such places.

It happens at a time when shame and disgrace are their best companions. Stupid Friends will take you to places where stupid things will happen to you.

Instead of letting Stupid Friends control our lives, it is my prayer that all of us will learn to make good decisions, to drop these sorts of people, and to move forward in our lives.

If you have Stupid Friends, please do yourself a favor and get rid of them before they make you stupid. They have a way of making you do stupid things to mess up your good life.

You do not have to let Stupid Friends mess up your life; it is a choice. Watch out for Stupid Friends! Drop the Stuff.

Chapter 8: Bad Places

I believe that not all places are good for us. There are some places we should not go. We are more likely to do immoral and illegal things at certain places.

These are the places we go to hide from our parents, spouses, family, friends, pastors, or bosses. We have certain secret behaviors that we do not want others to know about. Because we want to do illicit things, we find safe havens where no one will question or judge our morality.

Not all places I call Bad Places are actually bad. It is the things we do there that are bad; these places promote our ugly, secret behaviors.

For example, a friend's house where you drink, smoke, or meet with men or women is a Bad Place. A bar where you go to drink alcohol when you should not be drinking is a Bad Place.

A hotel room where you meet to have sex with someone who is not your spouse or where you take part in other illicit acts is a Bad Place. A corner where you meet to do illegal business is a Bad Place.

When we do away with the places we go to perform immoral and illegal affairs, we will generally cease those bad behaviors. In our quest to become more refined and productive, we must do all we can to stay away from such places.

Do you remember a place where you used to meet—or where you still meet—the person with whom you did/do that *thing*? You know what I am talking about; yes, it is okay to laugh. I bet you remember now.

Some of us go to certain places to attend meetings of secret societies and occult groups. In many parts of Liberia, most tribes have their own secret societies and venerate different things as gods.

In some places, men and women have separate secret societies in which the other gender cannot participate. Other societies are meant for both men and women.

Some of the commonly known secret societies in Liberia conduct female genital mutilation. In many other secret societies, people are given things to swallow as a means of buying their silence; talking secrets will only bring untimely death, or at least the fear of death.

Meetings for secret societies in rural areas, kidnappings and the selling of spare body parts in cities—all are bad things. Such places and the things that happen there bring crippling fear upon society.

Sadly, in some places in Liberia, it's said that for one to be a leader, one must attend these secret society meetings. Some of these societies require their members to bring a victim for human sacrifice.

Must we really go to such places to secure leadership positions? I do not think so, yet it happens.

Sometimes pressing conditions make people believe that they must attend secret meetings and pay dues if they are to become somebody in society; this is not true.

If you are from Liberia, you may know about how the occult kills people and takes their body parts. The things people do in secret—dismantling innocent people—can be horrendous. I do not think this wickedness is the only way of life.

Not all evils involve the occult and the extraction of human body parts; sometimes people decide the fate of a nation, business, or group of people behind closed doors or in open squares at midnight. There are illegal and immoral things associated with some places; stay away from those places.

In some places, people in secret societies decide on a nation's destiny under cover of darkness. This is so terrible.

When local or national leadership is immoral, innocent citizens suffer the consequences. It can be difficult for them to bring about development because, when they do, all eyes are upon them.

Instead of working for the country and its citizens, leaders distribute national funds to annuities and use trust funds for themselves and their progeny while the masses go without jobs, food, electricity, water, sanitation, education, and healthcare. What people do in Bad Places is unimaginable! It is just horrible.

Some of us who do not go to Bad Places still do bad things. As you read the previous lines, perhaps you had a grin on your face or even smiled as you said in your heart, *"But for me, I do not go anywhere."* Yes, you may be quite correct.

This is the next thing I want to address. Some of us do not go to Bad Places to do bad things; we just convert good places—like our homes, friend's homes, workplaces, parks, and even religious places—into Bad Places.

While you may enjoy the comfort of a good place under the open sun or under the cover of darkness, it really does not matter; what matters is what you do there.

Many people across the globe have done so much evil to harm others in religious centers like churches and mosques. People have done so much evil to family members in the comfort of their homes. Across the globe, at an alarming rate, women are molested in friendly environments by so-called family or friends. Sadly, most of these cases are not reported because those concerned protect the perpetrators due to their connections; the crime is kept a family secret, to the detriment of the victims. I think that such people must receive a harsh punishment for taking advantage of people whom they called family or friends. This is so wrong and unfair.

When we change the meaning of a place to suit our evil ambitions, we corrupt the good place and, in that moment, make it a Bad Place.

Whether it is a church, strip club, hotel room, or ghetto area, wherever we do bad things, the evils we plot can harm us and many other people.

I challenge you today to stop going to Bad Places to do bad things. I urge you to stop converting good places into places of evil. When we do such things, we deceive ourselves and bring harm upon others.

I challenge you today to pursue a moral life that will benefit you and everyone connected to you.

There is something special about you, but that Bad Place has corrupted you and turned you into someone you are not. We need you. Please desist from any bad practices and be a good person. There is more to life than that.

Drop the Stuff.

Chapter 9: Extra Load

When people enter into serious relationships like love, work, and business, they usually talk about the nature of those relationships. They discuss the dos and don'ts and the expectancy of their bond. With mutual understanding of roles and obligations, the relationship can begin.

Some people or businesses develop in-depth understandings of what is at stake and give all they have to make things work. Under such an atmosphere of mutual understanding and hard work, things turn out better for the people and organizations.

Many companies have lengthy orientations for new partners and employees, similar to the way many people court a member of the opposite sex for some time before they begin a serious relationship. Such courtships provide time to settle any issues that could ruin the relationship.

These things are done to safeguard the other person or the organization before somebody gets on board and does things contrary to what the person or organization stands for.

During such times, people learn important things about the other; their strengths and weaknesses are considered. Choices are made whether to abort or continue the friendship. In business, newcomers learn the philosophy and style of the organization, and get to understand the vision.

Despite the fact that all these things have been set in place to avoid assumptions, misunderstandings, or other problems, many people who enter into relationships or join organizations start operating totally contrary to what the person or group stands for.

After the company spent a lot of money on training, or after the other person opened his or her life, these people become a threat to the company's operations and to the very existence of the company or person.

In romantic relationships, people tell their partners sweet things and behave like little angels; however, later they reveal themselves to be the devil's incarnate. Why? Why would people come with an Extra Load we know nothing about? Why would they deceive us?

Most of the time if these deceitful people are asked why they did not discuss the Extra Load they brought onboard earlier, their answers bring chills. Some of them would say,

"I was afraid that if I told you, I would not be welcomed." Heck yeah! Who wants to mess up their life? Or *"I did it to protect you."*

Protect who?
They know that the Extra Load would be unacceptable; this is why they lied to us. For them, it was better to look us in the eye and blatantly lie with ease than to give us the opportunity to make our own decisions.

Is that how to patronize people or what? How could they think that they were protecting us when their Extra Load has wrecked our lives and brought us nothing but trouble? Why do people do this?

There are a few troubling stories about people bringing an Extra Load into other people's lives, trapping them and fostering misery. I will tell you a touching story.

There is a certain pastor in whose group it is taboo to discuss the issue of sex in public. The group keeps such discussions in the home and in private. This man gave his life to God later on in life.

Because of his devotion to God, he practiced chastity and decided not to mess around with women until he married. He became a very good pastor.

After some time in ministry, he found a beautiful lady who caught his heart. Soon after they began courting and dating; then, they married.

During their time of courtship, as a young couple-to-be, they talked about everything related to their new life together. They talked about the ministry, family projects, and education. They talked about internal issues like their love life and kids. Everything sounded promising. Discussion of their honeymoon brought them even more laughter; they were madly in love.

After a long wait, they got married. Then it was time for the honeymoon. Sadly, that is where problem number one began. The lady did not want to have sex.

At first the pastor thought it was just fear on her part, so he let her be and nothing happened the first night. Wow, pastor, I feel bad for you. I cannot imagine looking upon my beautiful new wife in bed, wearing her prized lingerie, and having to listen to some cockroach story. I applaud the pastor for his patience.

The next night, the same thing happened. This went on for the whole week. Every time the pastor brought up the discussion, his wife would get angry and talk to him harshly, saying things like,

"You are a pastor; aren't you supposed to be more concerned about prayer and ministry than talking about sex every day?"

She made him feel guilty for asking for sex—something every married couple should enjoy during their honeymoon without question. I think somebody needed to beat some sense into that lady's head! She's lucky it wasn't me.

If I were the pastor, I would have said to her, "Who says pastors do not have sex?" Hey, come on, stop laughing. It is not fair to use a person's faith against him in a twisted way. I wonder who told this lady that pastors' wives deny their husbands sex? From where did she get these stupid, crazy ideas? Why get married without planning to enjoy the whole package? It is not fair.

For our dear pastor, the problem of no sex continued for a year; though married, he never had the opportunity to consummate his marriage. Our dear pastor kept this thing to himself; he did not even tell his senior pastor for fear that his wife would be chastised or ridiculed. He just kept it in and asked God to help him in the situation.

In the middle of the second year of his marriage, another side of the story emerged. His wife, who had been refusing him sex for two years into their marriage, invited some family over for the weekend. The pastor and his in-laws had a good time together.

When the day came for them to leave, he gathered some things and gave them money to take to other relatives. As he bade them farewell, his wife called to him and said that they were not going anywhere.

To his surprise, this is what she said. "Those two kids who came here are actually my children. They are to live with us now since we are married."

Oh my goodness! The man was terribly shocked. He fell to the ground in a faint.

Neighbors were called and they rushed him to the hospital. When the doctors asked the wife what had happened, she told them that he just fell—nothing had really happened. This lady was a good liar.

Through the help of God and medical treatment, the pastor came to himself three days later. When his senior pastor visited, our dear pastor could not keep the secret any longer. He told his pastor about the sex starvation and the two kids. Everybody was surprised and in a great shock.

Now, let me ask you: Why would a woman married to a pastor refuse to have sex with him after their wedding? Why did she hide her two children?

By the way, I bet she had had sex multiple times before she conceived those kids with somebody else. Why, then, would she cause an innocent man to suffer this much? Wow! Some people are simply wicked. I leave the ending of the story to your imagination.

Do you think the pastor forgave her? Or do you think that he had grounds for divorce? If he forgave her, do you think she agreed to have sex with him? I would like to know what you think. This so-called "pastor's wife" was quite a wicked woman. She brought Extra Loads: No Sex and Two Kids! Yeah, those were really big loads. Do you think you would have waited that long for sex after marriage when the woman had no health problems? As for myself, I do not think so, but I applaud this strong pastor.

Every day across the globe, people join organizations or join the lives of others only to bring with them things that wreak havoc on the organizations and people.

I think it is a good thing to tell the truth and not act out of our selfish ambitions. To do otherwise is sheer wickedness.

When we are open about who we are and what we can bring to the table, transparency occurs and proves that we are honest. Hidden agendas, when discovered, only cause problems.

It is better to say it out loud; perhaps the other person or organization would welcome you regardless. I encourage you today to be upfront with people and to not bring along the Extra Load they did not sign up for. Do not do this, please.

How will we know that we have changed and how will others know that we have Dropped the Stuff? It is simple. The Bible says the following about false prophets and all those who pretend to be something they are not,

[53]By their fruit you will recognize them. [Matthew 7:20]

It is your choice; you can drop that stuff. You leave behind the Stinking Thinking, Stupid Friends, and Bad Places and enter a more rewarding and fulfilling life. It is your choice. All you have to do is Drop the Stuff.

It is my prayer that each us will examine ourselves and see the obvious people, things, and places that are keeping us down. Better yet, let us look a little deeper to see inside ourselves the things other people do not see; such things can have detrimental effects.

Let us dig deep inside our hearts and carefully consider anything that might stand in the way of our success. Others are advancing, and I do not think you deserve to be left behind. Do not celebrate yesterday when we are living in today and preparing for a brighter tomorrow. Drop the Stuff!

PART FOUR:
Born to Take Charge

God has given us a five-fold duty charge at the dawn of creation to:

- Be Fruitful
- Multiply
- Fill the Earth
- Subdue it, and
- Have Dominion

This call to duty tells us the reason we were created. It gives purpose and meaning to life. Regardless of race, color, status, and location, we are all charged with a responsibility to leadership.

There are three classes of people. The first class has done well. The people in this class have made our lives better in many ways. People in the second class are those who try hard every day to make an impact. They have not been able to do something tangible yet, but they are determined not to give up until something good happens.

In the third class are the people have done nothing. They just eat and live off of what others have done. They sit back and do nothing except complain about how everything is.

So let me ask you: Where do you find yourself today? Are you among the champions and world changers, the people who are trying hard to make it, or the consumers who aren't productive?

We are Born to Take Charge. We should work hard and make our world a better place for everyone. We must improve human relations, science, and technology. We must take part in charity. It is not time to sit back and do nothing. All of us should get busy doing something. The world is calling.

Chapter 10: Five-Fold Duty Charge

I want all of us to understand that God is. I want to address those of you who want proof of God's existence before you'll believe that God is.

It is not that you do not believe that God is, but rather that you do not know how to fit God into your worldview. In your mind, you have explanations for all natural occurrences.

For the ones you cannot explain, you rely on scientific guesses that the occurrences must have happened due to interactions between molecules and atoms throughout the course of millions of years. Before you brush this off, let me use examples to explain.

It took scientists many years to discover that the earth was not flat or that it doesn't have four corners; instead, the earth is somewhat round. It took time before scientists discovered the planets and even more time before man went to the moon and sent machines to Mars and deep space.

It took extensive research before scientists discovered penicillin and many other antibiotics and vaccines. It took man a long time to invent vehicles and airplanes.

What were the answers we used to explain these things before their discovery? And what do we say to people today who do not believe in good science and still think of things the way people did in ages past?

You see, our ignorance or denial about a person, place, or thing does not negate its reality and impact.

When we consider the sophistication of the human mind, which operates like a heavy-duty computer, we must conclude that a designer is behind this magnificent work.

Look at planet earth; the way it lives suggests a designer. Consider the seasons, the topography, the seas and oceans, the clouds and winds; the way they come and go in their seasons points to one conclusion—the existence of a designer.

There is a designer who put the planets together in their orbits. It is the same designer who composed the stars, moons, and host of galaxies, both known and unknown. Everything serves a purpose; if one planet or moon or asteroid were to change its position, it would cause chaos, both up there and down here.

There are a few questions we must think about. How are these things kept together in space? Did they arise out of nowhere and put themselves in place because they attracted each other? Before we can say all this, please consider the following.

How did the universe, which looks like a multi-verse, start? Where did the first atom, molecule, particle, or gas come from? What was its composition and how did it arrive there? When we begin to ask these questions, we go beyond science and enter the realm of philosophy and religion.

Science deals with proven data and does not necessarily make faith statements. So if we want to use science alone to prove the existence or non-existence of God, we have a long way to go.

Talk about God is an expression of faith. We must believe that God is; when we do, we get to know him personally and discover all the good plans he has for us. More people reject the notion of the call of God because of their morality. They hate rules.

They do not want anyone to question their morality or consider the possibility of some god holding them accountable for their dealings. If we could serve God without any rules, I really do think that a lot of people would find God easily and the fight would not persist. Now let's get back to our discussion.

The Bible declares that,

[54]*In the beginning God created the heavens and the earth.* [Genesis 1:1]

All created things have a creator and a purpose for their creation. Think about vehicles; they are made to transport people and things. There are different types of vehicles, and their operations, comfort, horsepower, size, and durability depend on their purpose.

When God made us, he gave us a purpose that we must accomplish. Sadly, many people have not discovered their purpose. If they do not know their purpose, how can they reach their destiny?

The writer of Genesis spoke of the creation story when he said:

[55]Then God said, "Let us make mankind in our image, in our likeness, so that they may rule over the fish in the sea and the birds in the sky, over the livestock and all the wild animals, and over all the creatures that move along the ground." [27]So God created mankind in his own image, in the image of God he created them; male and female he created them. [Genesis 1:26-27]

God made mankind in his image and likeness. That means that we are like God in beauty, character, and purpose. God is beautiful; he makes everything beautiful. God has character—a way to love and care about us and maintain everything else for our good.

God has a purpose; he does things for a reason. He created all things for his glory and for our comfort. Then God gave man dominion in the three spheres: land, air, and water.

This is why we are able to work the land, water, and air to discover new things every day; we have power over these things.

In the known creation, man is the most intelligent being; that is why we can tame the other animals. We can affect things in the sky. There are a lot of satellites in the sky for military and civilian use. We can use GPS to locate the positions of people and things anywhere around the globe.

Have you heard of HAARP? Look it up online. Whether it is true or not, this thing seems to have some special world-altering power.

HAARP is device in Alaska and other places around the world that is said to have the capacity to produce enough electricity to affect the weather, causing rain, storms, and earthquakes. It is said that HAARP can blow a hole in the ozone level and cause violent sun rays that will affect plants and animals on earth.

Whether or not this is another conspiracy theory, a lot is floating around these days concerning strange lines in the skies from planes that create rain and storms.

I bring this up to say that man is intelligent and can create and alter things. Man can create things that kill him and destroy his habitat. Do you remember Hiroshima and the atomic bomb? Man has grown smarter than that now.

God has given us the powers of imagination and creation. I hope you remember when I said earlier that God made man in his image and likeness and gave him dominion over creation.

Therefore, like God, we think things into action. Believers and unbelievers apply faith every day in logic, science, and religion, thereby imagining, forming, and creating things like our daddy—God.

I do not really see why some people refuse to accept and believe that God is, because every day we act like God in beauty, in character, and in purpose. God is.

In the next few pages we will discuss what I call the Five-Fold Duty Charge. Like soldiers who go to war, we must get a command and a "go" before we can enter the battlefield and face the enemy.

At the dawn of creation, before any mishaps, God gave man the charge to Be Fruitful, Multiply; Fill the Earth, Subdue It, and Have Dominion over the land, the waters, and the air. In short, man controls his new habitat.

We were given the undeniable right to rule our world, tame our world, and alter our world, but, sadly, we have also used the same knowledge to destroy our world. We must do all good things. Let us build instead of destroy.

Chapter 11: Born to Bear Fruit

We are not born to be useless. We are not born to be vagabonds. We are born to bear fruit, and not just any fruit, but good fruit.

The writer of Genesis teaches us that, in the beginning,

> [56]*So God created mankind in his own image, in the image of God he created them; male and female he created them. God blessed them and said to them, "Be fruitful and increase in number."* [Genesis 1:27-28a]

We should understand that each of us has something to produce. We all have the innate tendency to do something, make something, and improve on something. This is because God, the Creator of the heavens and the earth, fashioned us this way. We were born to Bear Fruit.

To Bear Fruit means that we must do something meaningful with our lives and give something to society. The degree of fruit-bearing varies according to certain factors. For example, the way we were physically born, our parents, our location, our upbringing—these in themselves do not totally prevent us from fulfilling our duties, though they could somehow play a role.

I understand that our parents, the places we were born, and our upbringing affect our lives. However, even if we were born under unfortunate circumstances and grew up in bad neighborhoods, we can still Bear Fruit.

We should arise from our limitations and fight our way toward becoming productive citizens in spite of the pressing opposition we might face. There are some people who take pleasure in the depravity of the poor and unfortunate people in society.

The truth is, some people have created systems to keep the poor man poor so that they can feel important. They want the poor to remain in abject poverty so that after they have made their millions, they can make a show of taking part in some benevolent act for tax breaks.

They create systems to maintain poverty as a way of proving that color and status matter. Some people do not want minorities to get ahead in life, so they create road blocks.

I am here to tell you that, in spite of what the western world has done to rid society of discrimination, the sad truth is that discrimination does exist.

Every day we see discrimination in Black America. Every day we see discrimination against various minority groups in America, and even in Europe and other places in which it has been outlawed.

But who condemns such actions when they come from the top, covered in heavy secrecy and red tape. Everyone in the mainstream media understands these actions, but no one dares talk about them. Certain people create these systems so that other people can do the dirty work while the leaders sip red wine in ballrooms.

Everyone acts as though they do not know what is going on. As a matter of fact, some of them have to talk about it and against it; sometimes they do things to appease the public, but deep down in their hearts they know that they are the ones who have created such terrible systems, which deny certain people of the benefits of life.

They have created systems to limit some people and push others to higher heights. Oh my goodness! May God help us reexamine our moralities!

It is no wonder that people do not want God these days. Talk of God brings about the issue of morality, which they do not want to be bothered with. This needs to change. It is my prayer that God will intervene.

Who says nothing good can come from the ghetto? No, ghetto dwellers do not have to live down to the expectations of the affluent and the powerful. They cannot continue living like people without brains, destitute and standing in line for rations. They, too, have a voice and a future. As a matter of fact, I believe that rations systems have prevented the advancement of minorities. To qualify for rations, food stamps, and cash, some minorities remain jobless, work in low-paying jobs, and make plenty of babies. However, others are going to school and getting good jobs. It is the little they take from the affluent, a portion of their taxes that keeps them in a state of poverty and prevents them from achieving a certain status quo.

God has given us a charge to Bear Fruit. Let us not sit back and let others think that this charge applies only to them and that we cannot participate in this heavenly mandate. It is our inalienable, undeniable right. The same God who gave them the power and the will to do things that bear fruit is our God, too. Come on, rise up!

History has shown that good things can come from the ghetto. Good things have come from poor countries, and truly good things have come from unknown people.

We all have a divine calling to Bear Fruit. It is not something for the Americans, Europeans, Germans, Russians, Australians, Chinese, Koreans, and Japanese alone; Africans, Latinos, Native Americans, and people everywhere have received this divine mandate to Bear Fruit.

We cannot live like people who were created with different material. All of us were created by the same God. Let us not let geography, the lies of the West, or internal corruption damn us and rob us of the call to Bear Fruit.

On an individual level, some people are just lazy; they do not want to work. My grandpa told me,

"If you do not work, you do not eat."

One day I decided that I was too tired to work on the farm after school. My grandpa was not angry. As he picked up his cutlass, in a very soft voice he said those words to me. Though I was a little boy at the time, those words continue to ring in my ears today: "No work, no food."

As I grew into a man, I began to understand that things do not simply come free. People work for things; even if they are given as gifts, someone somewhere worked to earn them.

The Bible tells us the story of the Fall of Man, when God told Adam,

[57]*By the sweat of your brow you will eat your food until you return to the ground, since from it you were taken; for dust you are and to dust you will return.* [Genesis 3:19]

In life, we must work to eat. Work is work. Whether we use our brains or we labor with our bodies, all of us must work. In today's world, a few people are heirs to fortunes in the millions and billions; these people do not necessarily need to work because everything is already lined up for them. However, that is not so for most of us. We must work.

To live, people have to learn something, do something, work for somebody, or invent something. King Solomon said that,

[58]*Lazy hands make for poverty, but diligent hands bring wealth.* [Proverbs 10:4]

This is so true. We must all work with our brains and our bodies. Lazy people make room for poverty but hard work brings wealth. It is no surprise that King Solomon again said that,

[59]*The lazy man does not roast his game, but the diligent man prizes his possessions.* [Proverbs 12:27]

Some people do not know the value of the things they have. They treat valuable things and people any way they want.

Good luck does not always arrive as many promise; the day heaven shines on us and brings us something, or when someone takes us to the next level to change our situation, we must treat them like royalty.

When we are lazy, we might become stupid. We throw good things to the floor, yet we cry for help. It does not have to be so; we can all change.

In this world, life is all about performance. People want to know what we can produce, what we can bring to the table. They want to know what fruit we can bear. There is a stage set in relationships and it is something like this: "You want me? Okay, yes, I agree. But what can you bring? What can you do for me? What fruit can you bear that will not just take away from me, but add on to what I have?"

During job interviews, candidates are asked, should they be hired, what they will bring to the company. In sports, players are expected to perform. In production lines, people must prove that they can do the job. In the military, soldiers must prove their solidarity to their country and defend it with their lives. They must bear fruit, especially on the battlefield.

Religious people are expected to Bear Fruit, as Jesus said,

[60]Thus, by their fruit you will recognize them. [Matthew 7:20]

Preachers in churches must Bear Fruit. Church leaders and church workers must all Bear Fruit. They must understand that church is like a platform for performance. Every day they must prove that God is God in all situations, and their words and deeds must match their beliefs. They must not try to fool society by hiding behind religion.

Students everywhere must Bear Fruit by getting good grades and conduct themselves morally. Justice departments in all countries must Bear Fruit and administer justice without discrimination.

Businesses must Bear Fruit by producing good products and services. We are all called to Bear Fruit; none of us have an excuse as to why we cannot Bear Fruit.

I have come with a deep conviction that God did not create us simply to Bear Fruit, but to Bear Good Fruit. Our performance must be optimal; our production must not be good, but very good.

It is not simply about bearing any fruit; we must give something better to society. Each of us has a signature.

Let the world know that James Nyemah did it. Let the world know that you did it because you have your own style and class that distinguishes you from others. You are class. You are dignity. Live it.

We must Bear Fruit that we are proud of. We must understand that in life there is competition and that, sadly, not all the competitors play by the rules. Some people love to cheat or step on others.

Therefore, we must play hard and play smart. Our production must beat the competitor's by a wide margin beyond any reasonable doubt.

Aha! I can hear somebody saying that I demand too much. I want perfection. No, no, no; not that. It is not like that, but we must give our best in life. We are sophisticated people with class. Our productions must be good, very good.

When we produce something good and durable, it sells. Our lifestyles and products are things people long for. We must give society nothing short of the very best.

It is my prayer that all of us live our lives and Bear Fruit. No food for lazy men; you must remember that. Every person must find something to do and try his or her best so that through our efforts God can show us favor and bless our work. God wants all of us to Bear Fruit. God does not want us to sit around and cry or wait in lines for rations when we can go out and help ourselves. It is better to lick your own hand than to lick somebody else's hands after they themselves have licked their hands clean.

My dear brothers and sisters, please understand that we are called to Bear Fruit. Interestingly, what we are signifies what we offer. Jesus, in teaching the people, said,

[61]A good tree cannot bear bad fruit, and a bad tree cannot bear good fruit. Every tree that does not bear good fruit is cut down and thrown into the fire. [Matthew 7:18-19]

If we say that we are good people, we must bear good fruit. As good trees bear good fruit, we are to bear good fruit. When good trees bear bad fruit, they are usually cut down and thrown into the fire. What does this mean? When we do not Bear Fruit or produce anything good, people usually turn their backs on us and forget about us. When this happens, our lives can be reduced to nothing and we fade away into obscurity.

It is easier to do something and Bear Fruit than to face the pains of being forgotten and having our lives reduced to nothing. Please do not let others down; your parents and the community count on you. You have something to give.

I have something to give. You have something to give. Every one of us has something special, something with the capacity to lift us from one level to another. When we employ hard work and begin to Bear Fruit, when we produce good things and demonstrate our talents and abilities, God can bless our work and we become "somebody."

Today I challenge you to refrain from becoming a "nobody" when you can become a real "somebody" after whom people and companies will run.

Arise, discover your purpose. Live your purpose to reach your destiny. You are not a halfway passenger. You are not alive to remain in the shadows of other people. There is a stage set for you.

Arise and Bear Fruit, and not just any fruit, but good fruit. Bear irresistible eye-pleasing fruit. The world is waiting for you. Go on!

CHAPTER 12: BORN TO MULTIPLY

The Bible teaches us that in the beginning God said,

[62]Let us make mankind in our image, in our likeness. So God created mankind in his own image, in the image of God he created them; male and female he created them. And God blessed them, and God said unto them, "Be fruitful, and Multiply." [Genesis 1:26a, 27, 28a]

I want you to understand that we were Born to Be Fruitful; we were Born to Multiply. A mango seed, when planted, comes forth and grows up to be a mango tree; the mango tree bears many fruits in its season. When a mango tree bears fruit, it does not bear only one; instead, it bears hundreds of mangoes.

Like a mango seed that grows and multiplies into hundreds of mangoes in its season, God wants us to bear much fruit and multiply. Seeds in the wild bring forth more fruits and more seeds in a single fruit than the one seed that was planted.

Moreover, humans must Multiply in our fruit bearing. God does not want us to remain the same; he wants us to grow and Multiply.

We are Born to Multiply.

It is not an increase in addition, but in multiplication because addition is too slow for us.

We are very smart people. We do great things. We calculate better. We analyze, we forecast, we deeply examine things. We are that good. This is why we can skip the primary growth of addition and jump straight to multiplication; we deserve more. You deserve better.

As a matter of fact, God wants us to Multiply Exponentially. We are fashioned in a unique way that allows us to use our challenges and oppositions as opportunities for growth and advancement. We are not moribund. We are not motionless. We are mobile. We are replicable. We can branch out into other auxiliaries and divisions that will bear our names.

This increase is not limited to business, but also extends to education, health, sports, innovation, organizations, social relations, and personal affairs. God wants us to multiply in every area of our lives.

We were not set up to be in one place; we have an innate tendency, an inborn desire, to grow and spread.

That is why in businesses we can have one store and build another. We can have multiple divisions, multiple labels under one umbrella.

God said the following to the children of Israel,

[63]*Little by little I will drive them out from before you, until you have increased, and you inherit the land.* [Exodus 23:20]

We were Born to Multiply, and the good news is that God himself will help remove stumbling blocks in our way. Many of us should have been established and known by now, but for some reason, things in our paths have limited us and cornered us so that we cannot move any farther.

It seems as though we have not done much to get out of the situation and bring about an increase, make a profit, or simply lead. The truth is, some of us have done a lot, but nothing seems to work.

Well, I have good advice for you: try God. When talking with the disciples who fished all night without catching anything, Jesus said,

[64]*"Throw your net on the right side of the boat and you will find some."* [John 21:6]

When they did, they couldn't haul in the net because of the large number of fish they had caught. I am not here to challenge your expertise and strategies, but I am here to tell you one simple thing: try God.

Even though the disciples were professional fishermen, they fished all night without a catch. At the word of Jesus, they reaped a great catch.

We can trust God regardless of our professionalism. There are times when even our professionalism and best strategies fail us; yes, it happens every day. In spite of who we are and what we know, we must learn to trust the Master.

You don't have to be a fisherman to catch fish; the concept applies to all areas of our lives. When you try God and when I try God, we all discover that he is alright.

Increase by multiplication comes from God. In all our dealings, let us not forget that he has ordained our success.

It is very important that we be mindful about the increase God brings. The multiplication and prosperity we receive must be handled with care because others revel in our times of loss, defeat, and demise. They want to destroy us.

In simple words, some people do not want you to have anything good; they wish you were dead. They may laugh with you, but deep down within their hearts they harbor hatred. They want to hear that your business failed; they want to hear that you lost everything. Do not let thoughts of them incapacitate you. Do your thing.

Some people do not want anything good to come from us; that is why we must be careful. The writer of Genesis said:

[65]*And he said to them, "Do not hinder me, since the Lord has prospered my way; send me away so that I may go to my master."* [Genesis 24:56]

Some people want to delay our growth. They think that we are not good enough for good things. On our way to multiplication, we should not let anyone delay us.

When our time has come, we must maximize every opportunity. Good things do not always come easily. When our day of increase comes, let us cherish it and use it properly.

We must be mindful of our increase, as jealous and wicked people will want to plan evil against us because we are moving forward.

Job, a man in the Bible, once said:

[66]*Dreadful sounds are in his ears; in prosperity the destroyer comes upon him."* [Job 15:21]

Out of envy, wicked people plan to rob us and kill us because of our things. When they see that we are increasing, evil enters their minds.

When we increase and multiply in business and everything else, we must ask God to give us the wisdom we need to take care of our businesses, partners, and property.

We must learn how to protect and insure them against any eventualities. When we are growing and multiplying, we should not sit back and risk everything. We must have security, insurance, and some sort of damage control strategy. Good things do not come easily for everyone. If heaven shines on us, we should use the opportunity wisely.

Why do we need to multiply? The reason is simple: our lives depend on it. The times are changing; new technologies and developments emerge daily. If we do not grow, it will not be long before our products and ideas become obsolete.

In growth, we devise new ways to remain competitive and offer fresh goods and services that consumers want. For example, in times past, landlines were good, but nowadays almost everyone has a smartphone. If your business is selling traditional landlines, you are out of luck because most people don't want that service anymore.

As time pushes forth demands, we must innovate and produce goods and services that consumers want. If we do not do that, we will fade away. It is my prayer that God will help all of us get the edge and Multiply in all we do.

Remember, God says Multiply. It is a command that we must obey. We were Born to Multiply; multiply today exponentially!

Chapter 13: Born to Fill the Earth

The call to Fill the Earth is similar to the call to Multiply, but they are not the same thing. I know that plenty of smart people just asked, "Are they not both talking about increase and growth?" Oh yes, you are right in that they both talk about increase, but there is a dissimilarity in size and magnitude. God could have easily said one or the other, but he said both. Let me use an example to explain the difference.

In my country, Liberia, many people own rice farms, but not many can produce a quantity large enough to sell on a town or county level, much less on a national level.

The size of these farms is relatively small. The farms are good only for feeding the owners' families. Because of the farms' capacity, the owners can never dream of exporting rice. If they cannot feed their towns, cities, counties, or small country, how can they even think about selling rice to other countries? Some of these owners may have the largest rice farms in their towns; they may even have enough to sell in town, but not enough to sustain local demand.

Let's link this to multiplication and filling the earth. Our growth may be noticeable in our little area, but God has a much bigger agenda that will carry us countywide, statewide, countrywide, and, in fact, across the world!

Nobody said that we cannot send our goods and services to the international market, where people are paying more for what we have! Nobody said that we cannot grow, multiply, and fill the earth!

Nobody said that your business, your products, your services, your organization, your ministry, your church, or your company cannot get big! I say this with an exclamation because so many of us think so little of ourselves and our capabilities when, in fact, there is a lot to us. We have limited ourselves as though we do not have what it takes to grow and excel. We can all advance from one level to the next. We have what it takes.

I have come here today to declare the word of the Lord upon your life, that you will be Fruitful. You will Multiply. And, quite frankly, you will Fill the Earth.

You cannot subject yourself to limitations. God will open your mind and give you creativity and innovation that will lead you to a broader audience or more customers. The writer of Genesis spoke the following of Isaac,

[67]*The man began to prosper, and continued prospering until he became very prosperous.* [Genesis 26:13]

What is this passage saying? Isaac's growth became exponential; he began to grow and grow until he became very prosperous. In other words, he became a multi-billionaire.

God wants to bless us and extend our territories. God wants us to be recognized by what we know and do. We are not simply sidewalk musicians; a stage is out there awaiting us. Your product can sell; your idea can sell, even on the international market.

Job, a man in the Bible, said that,

[68]*If they obey and serve Him, They shall spend their days in prosperity, and their years in pleasures.* [Job 36:11]

What was Job saying? Recognition of God, the Creator, in our lives can bring us prosperity. Serving the Lord can bring us prosperity. God knows how to give good gifts to his children and wants all of us to have plenty.

In whatever we do, God wants us to grow and multiply. He desires not just growth in our little areas, but growth that will put us in the headlines.

We must ask ourselves a simple question. If others are excelling in life, why aren't we? What do those people have that we do not? What are they doing that we are not doing? What strategies do they apply that we have not yet discovered?

When we are confronted with stagnation, these are all valid questions for the soul. I am here to encourage you. We can all start from where we are now. We can ask God to direct us in all our endeavors.

It is a good thing when we look at our work and thank all those who helped us reach where we are today.

You see, some of the people we overlook hold the keys to our uplifting. Showing them proper appreciation will help us relinquish their hold on our lives so that we can move into the next level of recognizable growth.

Some of us have a rough time and struggle in everything we do; others do not know the meaning of the words "poverty" or "lack." Maybe they were born into plenty or grew up in the midst of plenty or they make serious money; they always have everything they want. The money that they spend on pastimes equals our annual salaries.

King David once said that,

[69]*He himself shall dwell in prosperity, and his descendants shall inherit the earth.* [Psalm 25:13]

There are people who have enjoyed good things and are so blessed and rich that their children, grandchildren, and other descendants can live in prosperity for a century. In simple words: they are stinking rich.

Let me put it this way; instead of running the one or two shops or beauty salons or service centers in your city; you can do more. You can do more.

When you Multiply you will have more branches, but when you Fill the Earth, you will have a franchise or network of stores, shops, salons, service centers, and conglomerates. Your goods and services will cover the region. Your brand name will be known; people will recognize you for what you are worth.

When you Fill the Earth, God gives you your own stage on which to operate. You are meant to do more than stand in the shadow of another person all your life. You can graduate from that and move to the next level and to the level after that; this is what I mean when I say "Fill the Earth."

Let people talk about you. Let those who have nothing better to do gossip about your new development. Guess what? The more they talk, the more they gossip, the more you go higher and higher and higher!

Many people have great ideas and offer wonderful goods and services, but they are still poor; nobody knows about them. When you Fill the Earth, you become the talk of the town.

Radio talk shows and the social media will carry the news about your goods and services. They will carry the news about your ministry or church. You can surely be prosperous and prosperous and prosperous!

Such prosperity is not a white man's thing; it is not about the Koreans or the Chinese or the Japanese. It can be about Africans, Latinos, minorities, and people in third-world countries as well.

The blessings of God are indiscriminate to color, size, age, location, or social background. In the eyes of God, we are all equal. Whatever God does for the white man, he can do for the black man and the brown man and, of course, the yellow man.

God can bless not just the Westerner, but also the black man and the Latino, the Indian and the Islander. Each of us must prepare ourselves to receive these blessings.

We must all work hard. Remember, there is no food for the lazy man. We cannot sit back and expect riches to fall into our laps. Unless we have a rich family, we must work. It is hard work and the application of good strategy that will elevate us; faith and prayer become vital.

God did not make us simply so we could exist; no! We are Born to Fill the Earth. When couples have kids, those kids must grow from one level of maturity to another until they are mature enough to be on their own.

At that point, they must chart their own course in life and find something meaningful to do. We do not expect that they will constantly struggle and barely survive from paycheck to paycheck. If they have a job, we want them to excel. We expect them to become important figures in society.

We expect them to gain expertise in their professions and to make things happen. In the same way, God expects us to become the movers and shakers of society. We can change things for the better. We are Born to Fill the Earth; let us fulfill our destiny.

Chapter 14: Born to Subdue

God knows that when we obey his command to "Be Fruitful, Multiply, and Fill the Earth," we will face opposition. Our success has a way of attracting jealous, envious, and wicked people. It attracts those who want to bring us down.

They want to bring us down because they cannot stand our success. They are intimidated by our presence. They develop hatred and plot every way to tempt us, try us, and, of course, attack us directly. God knew this would happen; that is why he issued another command, which we are going to discuss now.

The Bible declares that when God made man, God blessed him and said to him,

[70]Be fruitful and increase in number; fill the earth and subdue it. [Genesis 1:28b]

God is quite aware of the opposition that will come our way. He expects us to mount our courage and face it. When God commanded us to bear fruit, increase, and grow beyond limitations, he also said that we should stand up to our foes and beat them down.

God expects us to Subdue the opposition. He has given us everything we need to live, enjoy life, and protect what we have from intruders.

We must know that,

[71]His divine power has given us everything we need for a godly life through our knowledge of him who called us. [II Peter 1:3]

God has given us everything we need, including the power to overcome the people and things that stand in our way or that want to destroy us.

Some people and things delay us; others rob us of our future, while still others simply want to kill us lest we try to get up again. When doing evil, people can be wicked and relentless.

The Psalmist understood God's empowerment and protection when he said,

⁷²You armed me with strength for battle; you humbled my adversaries before me. [Psalm 18:39]

In other places, this is translated as "You subdue my enemies under my feet." I like that.

The Bible declares that God knows the end in the beginning, before the start of anything. On account of that, he knows that our prosperous lives will make others hate us.

God gave us strength to face our fiercest opposition. He can level our enemies before us. All we need to do is trust in his divine providence and follow his plan.

God spoke to us through the prophet Jeremiah when he said,

*⁷³"For I know the plans I have for you," declares the L*ORD*, "plans to prosper you and not to harm you, plans to give you hope and a future."* [Jeremiah 29:11]

God has great plans for each one of us. His plan for me is different from his plan for you. This is why we do not all like the same things. We choose a variety of professions and vocations because his plans are personal, unique, and distinctive to each person. I love this.

Because of his desire for us to prosper, and because his plan involves giving us hope and a future, he has armed us with strength for the battle. When the enemy comes to steal or kill or ultimately destroy us, God wants us to fight for what rightfully belongs to us.

We cannot let our businesses, communities, organizations, children, friends, and churches be destroyed by evildoers while we fold our hands or run away in fear. No way; we should fight the good fight to protect what we have.

Talking to the people one day, Jesus said the following about the devil,

⁷⁴The thief comes only to steal and kill and destroy; I have come that they may have life, and have it to the full. [John 10:10]

The devil is called the thief here because he is the mastermind thief. He knows how best to scam us—by giving us cheap things so that we will be distracted when he robs us of more valuable things. He steals our lives for lies.

The thief's mission is not to be our friend; far from it. He comes to steal what we have, kill our dreams and aspirations for life, and ultimately destroy our present and future. He is tactical. He is armed and dangerous.

Some people are alive but look dead because their lives have lost meaning and fulfillment. It seems as though they are simply going through the motions because they have lost the very reason to exist. This is what the devil can do to us if we do not stand up for our people and things.

We must know that we face opposition not necessarily because we did something wrong. No; it is because we simply exist. Now you tell me; should we give up our right to exist because of something or somebody? I do not think so.

We must be ready at all times to fight for who we are and what we have. We should not let anybody or any situation take advantage of us, as though we are not good enough to enjoy the good things in life.

Success in life is not intended for just a few elites in society; all of us can enjoy the good life. While our level of fulfillment and success varies, we can each enjoy life in our own little way without being bullied.

There are many parents who sit back and fold their hands as they watch their kids being destroyed by bad friends, drugs, alcohol, and pornography.

Instead of fighting for their own flesh and blood, they let so-called *"human rights and freedom"* destroy the very people and things that matter most.

In their laziness and misunderstanding of rights and freedom, they let promising kids destroy themselves. I challenge parents everywhere to fight for their kids; do not let bad people or addictions destroy them.

Some people sit back and let their relationships of many years slip out of their hands, victims of interlopers who were not there in the beginning. After years of struggle, now that the person's significant other is "somebody," another individual wants to claim him or her. No way!

Why would any man or woman sit back and let some loser take away his or her spouse? Come on, stand up for what is right; stand up for what belongs to you.

Do not let a loser steal your future so easily, as though you were a numbskull. If you love and care for your spouse, you must pray and take proper steps to keep the relationship going.

I know that in some relationships the other person leaves regardless of how wonderful his or her spouse is; this is an unfortunate part of life.

However, even in such circumstances, you must talk some sense into your spouse and deal with the other man or woman accordingly. If it is not worth it, do not bother.

If you have done all you can prayerfully and legally and your spouse still wants to go, I will say, let them go. God knows how to work justice and fight for you; please hold on. He will comfort you and lead you on your way. It may be hard for a while, but you will get over it.

In fighting for our people, things, and organizations, we must pray seriously because many times we face unseen spiritual components. Some of the issues require dialogue and legal advice.

When somebody wants to take what rightfully belongs to us, the worst thing to do is to sit back and do nothing. Even if we have enough, we must send a clear message to the person or organization that people cannot claim what is not theirs.

When we sit back, do nothing, and let the evil person or organization take what belongs to us, the person or organization might come back to take what belongs to our neighbors and other people.

If they can do it without opposition, trust me, they will come back and rub it in our faces. They will use people and properties in a way that affects our lives.

By the way, why would any rational human being sit back and let another person take advantage of him or her?

History has shown over and over that greedy people are never satisfied with what they have; they always want more. If we let them take what we have and they get away scot-free, they will always come back.

Do not let anyone insult your intelligence as though you were stupid; fight for what belongs to you, and the God of justice will help you. Do not let anyone bully you; come on, you are too big for that.

Fight for what belongs to you; if need be, fight for what belongs to those who have no one to talk for them. God will bless you.

Believers all over the world, you should be the ones championing the promises of God by defending what you and the people you love have. Do not let intruders raid your territory.

We should be fearless because God declares that:

[75]*No weapon forged against you will prevail, and you will refute every tongue that accuses you. This is the heritage of the servants of the Lord, and this is their vindication from me, declares the Lord.* [Isaiah 54:17]

We should not be useless Christians in our communities. We should not let the devil and corrupt people take everything that belongs to us. The God who made us and those evil people said that no weapon formed against us shall prosper because it is our heritage.

When we wake up in the morning, we should declare the word of God by saying, "'No weapon' fashioned against me, my family and friends, my job, my business, or my church shall prosper in Jesus's name."

In the midday, proclaim two words to the devil and the evil people: "no weapon." In the evening, before you go to bed, declare one more time, "'No weapon' shall touch us or prosper against us in the name of Jesus!"

As a matter of fact,

[76]*This is what the LORD says to his anointed, to Cyrus, whose right hand I take hold of to subdue nations before him and to strip kings of their armor, to open doors before him so that gates will not be shut.* [Isaiah 45:1]

Now I want you to cross a line through Cyrus and insert your name. Declare these words over your life. Say, "I will subdue nations and strip kings of their armor; open doors and gates will not shut; this is my heritage from the Lord." Yes, it is our heritage, our birthright.

We should not sit back and let evil people, corrupt people, mindless and heartless people enter our territory and take what belongs to us.

By the power of God in us, we will use every tool—prayer, mobilization, the law, the media, social outlets, and whatsoever is available—to defend our territory.

The sad reality is that we must deal with the oppositions we face in life. Sometimes we bring opposition upon ourselves through our words and deeds. In our shortcomings, we offend people; that can make others turn against us.

We all make mistakes; sometimes the consequences of our actions can become our worst opposition. We disobeyed people. We acted rude. We treated ourselves badly.

Even today, we cuss, we lie, and we cheat; sometimes we steal. Some of us have gossiped or lied about others. All our wrongdoings are catching up to us; this is the intrusion and the opposition we see today.

When we wrong others, we must put aside our stupid pride and ego and do the right things: apologize, make restitution, and sincerely promise not to do wrong again. We should stand by our words.

Many people do not like to admit their wrongs; instead, they find cheap excuses to defend themselves. Others admit their wrongs but do so only because they feel sorry for themselves; their words are not truly from their hearts.

Other people will apologize, but they do not want to make restitution and pay back what they took from their victims. They think that their empty words are enough, but they are wrong.

When we offend others, we must go all the way to say sorry, return anything we have taken, pay for any damages, and promise to never repeat our mistakes. This is the right way to settle things.

When we do this, we will avoid a lot of trouble tomorrow. If we do not, life has a way of turning around because the God of love is also the God of justice.

We will not go free forever after we damage others and leave them in pain and suffering. God is righteous and will pay each one of us according to our works. If the victims cannot get a payback, life has a way of making others retaliate against us without reason—all because of what we did to people in the past.

Please do not let your mistakes rob you of a better life; settle the matter and move on. In my country, Liberia, we have a proverb that says:

Small shame is better than big shame.

It is better to settle your matters in a timely manner than to let them compound upon each other. If you treat people poorly and do not settle the issue, God will exact justice upon you. Do not ever think that your evil against innocent people will go unnoticed.

The same God of love and forgiveness is the same God of justice.

However, there is good news for those of us who are weak. In our time of weakness, God has a plan for us.

Our God is not a perfectionist who expects that we will never sin or err; he knows our humanity and the presence of evil in this world. That is why the Bible speaks about God and says,

[77]*You will again have compassion on us; you will tread our sins underfoot and hurl all our iniquities into the depths of the sea.* [Micah 7:19]

For many of us, God must provide compassion and extra grace to the depths of the sea; otherwise, we will not survive a day. Some of us live simply to say sorry to others because we keep on doing stupid things.

It is my prayer that God will deliver us from any Stinking Thinking so that we can live lives of freedom and friendship. It is not good to keep doing wrong to family and friends. When we do so, we cause people to run from us; then loneliness and depression will become our new friends. I thank God for his compassion, grace, and mercy upon us in our sins and weaknesses; without him we cannot live.

Sometimes because of our status, our money, our family, our jobs, or our ministries, people try to take us down. They become jealous and plot against us in different ways, including by tempting us.

Why would people tempt us or set us up? The answer is simple: they want us to fail because of who we are and what we have. After they have tried techniques that do not work, they come at us with various temptations to make us fall off balance and miss the mark. They want to set us up for public ridicule.

The Apostle Paul, talking to the church in Corinth, said that,

[78]*These things happened to them as examples and were written down as warnings for us, on whom the culmination of the ages has come.* [I Corinthians 10:11]

If you think you are standing firm, be careful that you do not fall! No temptation has overtaken you except what is common to mankind. God is faithful; he will not let you be tempted beyond what you can bear. When you are tempted, he will provide a way out so that you can endure it.

Some things that happen serve as examples and warnings to us; in all our undertakings let us remember that it is God who gave us all things. Let us not become too ambitious and think that we arrived where we are on our own. Without God working behind the scenes and paving the way for us, we would not be where we are today. We should show God our gratitude.

We should also know that no temptation is new. When we face temptation, we must seek counsel from others to guide us.

We should understand that all the temptations that come our way are things we can overcome. However, it is a choice we must make and we must not celebrate our vulnerability. If we are not forced or pinned down or grossly blackmailed, we have a choice.

Even in case of blackmail, we may have some choices. We should not let fear overpower us. When temptation arrives, we can resist it or simply run from it before it destroys us.

Remember, it is we—not the others—who have something valuable to lose, so we must be careful. I thank God because the promise is that God will provide a way of escape for us.

It is up to us to resist the temptation or to run from it; if we allow it to take hold of us, we have only ourselves to blame.

When we face different oppositions in life, God wants us to take the right actions. He will be with us. If we did nothing wrong yet the devil still comes at us, we must fight and resist him. He will flee from us.

If we wronged others and things have now turned against us, we must fix the problem. If people tempt us and want to set us up so that we fail, we must not allow them to succeed. We must take appropriate actions and not let their worst get the best of us.

In any case, the Apostle Paul had this to say to the believers in Corinth:

[79]For though we live in the world, we do not wage war as the world does. The weapons we fight with are not the weapons of the world. On the contrary, they have divine power to demolish strongholds. We demolish arguments and every pretension that sets itself up against the knowledge of God, and we take captive every thought to make it obedient to Christ. And we will be ready to punish every act of disobedience, once your obedience is complete. [II Corinthians 10:3-6]

There are a few things we can learn from this passage. The first thing is that though we live here, we are not like everybody else. As individuals, we are different and unique.

We should act in ways befitting of us, exhibiting good conduct and maturity. We should not act like mindless brutes; we are better than that.

The next thing to understand is that we have good weapons against the opposition. We have our divine heritage and legal rights to existence and ownership. In addition to this, we have God.

With God, human connections, legal systems, good thinking, and the right attitude, we can overcome any opposition.

We can demolish arguments and pretensions. I do not like people who live lies and pretend to be things they are not. I do not know why they go through all of the trouble of lying about and showing off a lifestyle they do not have. It is a sad and terrible thing. I do not like people who pretend to be family and friends, but come only to steal and destroy. They do not desire genuine friendship. I hate that.

God commands us to take captive every thought, every inclination, every imagination, and anybody who opposes his good plan to help us prosper. We must take captive those things and people, subjecting them to the word of God.

We must tell the devil that he is a liar and we are who God says we are. We must tell the situation that it cannot get the best of us; no way. We must tell the people—the backbiters, the gossipers, the cheaters, the witches, and liars—that they cannot take enjoyment out of life for us. We must fight for what God has given us.

We must send the clear message that we are not easy prey. These people cannot simply reap from where they did not sow—no way.

God understands that the world is very full and that every human being is trying to make it in life. When we work hard to earn or inherit things, we have the right to keep and use them for our pleasure.

God knows that life is not easy. He will not simply sit back and let others take things that belong to us. God is a just God.

Today I want to encourage you to refrain from sitting back and letting your life be taken from you. God expects you to protect your own. He gave us the command to Be Fruitful, Multiply, Fill the Earth, and Subdue it.

The things you work for are yours; enjoy them. The things you inherit are yours; enjoy them gratefully. Do not let anyone take advantage of you when you have everything you need to win the battle against your opposition.

God has given us the power to overcome. Do not sit back and let your life be taken away from you while you watch. This is not a movie; it is your life. Fight for it. God bless you.

Chapter 15: Born to Have Dominion

Imagine what life would be like if we did not have any sort of control, power, and authority over things. I think it would be chaotic. A life of no law and order through which to define rules and regulations would be strange. With no rights and no ownership, life would be a total failure.

To have dominion means that you have power, control, or authority over a territory. In the beginning, when God made everything, he established confines, the boundaries of man's dominion.

The writer of Genesis talked about creation and the dominion of man when he said,

[80]*Then God said, "Let us make mankind in our image, in our likeness, so that they may rule over the fish in the sea and the birds in the sky, over the livestock and all the wild animals and over all the creatures that move along the ground."*

So God created mankind in his own image, in the image of God he created them; male and female he created them. God blessed them and said to them, "Be fruitful and increase in number; fill the earth and subdue it. Rule over the fish in the sea and the birds in the sky and over every living creature that moves on the ground." [Genesis 1:26-28]

According to this passage, we are created with a purpose in mind. We are not an accident; nor, as some would have us believe, are we the result of gasses, atoms, or molecules randomly bumping into each other over the course of millions of years.

We were created to be overseers and stewards of God's creation, starting with the earth. At creation, we were given a purpose. That purpose was to exert dominion over the things that fly in the air, the things that walk, hop, and crawl on the ground, and the things that dwell in the waters. In simple words, we have power over land, air, and water. That is why, in man's wisdom and constant imagination, we can create and make things to help us adjust, alter, and tame our environment.

Man has explored the world. Man is building machines to explore the planet in all its multiple facets and intricacies. Now man is moving on to things in our solar system and beyond. With boot prints and machines on the moon, as well as machines on Mars and other deep-space territories, man is doing his best to understand the world he has been put in charge of. Man has explored the waters and constantly conducts deep-sea explorations. Man has dug in and is still digging into the earth to uncover new knowledge every day.

With the advance in technology, deep space is the next big playground for man. Every country wants to do something in space. Whatever our curiosity desires, we want to fulfill it.

Why? Because God has put all things into our care so that we can tend and watch over them. I pray that as we dig into the earth and its moon, and as we travel to Mars and other planets and heavenly bodies, we will not cause irreversible damage. I hope that we will not one day kill ourselves in pursuit of knowledge.

I pray that our knowledge will not kill us, but that instead we will apply our scientific understanding with conscience and morality. The three actually make good company; without conscience and morality, we would push experiments to their limits until our own products took over the world.

One day, King David, king of Israel, began to wonder about the state of man. He said of God,

[81] *You have made them a little lower than the angels and crowned them with glory and honor.* [Psalm 8:5]

King David was amazed at the power, authority, and dominion that God has given man; man is lower than the angels, yet angels are servants to man. What a mystery!

In God's creation, man has a special place. God gave us an intellect that no other animal possesses; this is why we are able to tame the wild beasts for our pleasure.

We have control over the things in the air, on the ground, and in the waters. God said that we are capable of handling such authority; however, he expects much from us.

Dominion is good, but power, control, and authority is not good for everyone. Power in the hands of the wrong person can inflict pain and suffering upon the masses.

King Solomon, king of wisdom, once said,

[82]*When the righteous are in authority, the people rejoice: but when the wicked bears rule, the people mourn.* [Proverbs 29:2]

Oh, my brother Solomon, this is so true! People from oppressed and corrupt countries know what it means very well; they truly understand the pain and suffering marginalization can bring.

Countries in West Africa, such as Liberia, Ivory Coast, and Sierra Leone, as well as other places like Sudan, Somalia, and South Africa bear the scars of corrupt leadership.

A few people and their families, in-laws, friends, and special interests groups enjoy the country's resources while others cannot find work to provide for their families. These people lack decent sanitation, electricity, and clean water, yet corrupt leaders drive around town in luxury cars, eat at high-end restaurants, and sleep in the best hotels.

These leaders curb education, employment, health care, and social welfare for the common people while their own children travel out of the country to attend noted universities. They know how to enjoy life while their own countrymen suffer from and die of curable diseases. When these leaders or their family members are sick, they fly out of the country for the best medical care.

Their families and in-laws get the best jobs while others suffer extreme poverty. When power is in the hands of corrupt, self-seeking, greedy scavengers, only God can save his people!

I pray for God's divine intervention in places where the leadership is corrupt. It is my prayer that one day God will remove them from power in disgrace and will strip from them everything they have stolen from their countries.

I pray that God will give corrupt leaders a rude awakening like he did to King Nebuchadnezzar in the days of Daniel.

This is what the Scriptures said,

[83]Even as the words were on his lips, a voice came from heaven, "This is what is decreed for you, King Nebuchadnezzar: Your royal authority has been taken from you." [Daniel 4:31]

I pray that God will one day speak to all corrupt leaders and corrupt people like he did to this wicked king and remove them from their positions one by one.

I understand that when the leadership is corrupt, anyone who speaks the truth becomes an enemy of the state; the leaders want to silence people by bribes or by force.

They arrange killings or kidnappings at the hands of gangsters, who plant explosives in cars, offices, and houses to silence good people. If that is not possible, they accuse people and jail them without bail. I know how relentless corrupt leaders can be when protecting their eating grounds.

We can take civil actions that may result in casualties, but that will also inform the international community about the possible need for intervention; we must take the time to seriously pray about it.

Consider Dr. Martin Luther King, Jr. Talking alone was not enough; people had to put their words into action and perform their moral duties in spite of the cost, even at the loss of lives. Change is not easy. Freedom is not free! It takes sacrifice.

Prayer should never cease. We should pray that God will remove corrupt leaders from power so that development can occur in our countries and communities. This is not an easy, one-day thing; it takes serious talk and action. It takes sacrifice. Without prayer and civil action, we cannot end the rule of corruption.

On the other hand, when good people are in authority, the people truly rejoice. When you have authority and exercise your dominion accordingly, you do not have to talk for yourself. Everywhere you go, people will recognize you, as they did in the case of Jesus.

[84]The people were amazed at his teaching, because he taught them as one who had authority, not as the teachers of the law. [Mark 1:22]

The people were amazed at Jesus's teaching because he taught with authority, not with empty words forced upon them. When you rule properly, people will notice your honesty and freely fall under your dominion. They followed Jesus because his words produced good actions.

It is my prayer that leaders in our countries and communities will not lord their positions over the people, but instead that the people will recognize their honest, hard work. When leaders govern accordingly, people love and obey them everywhere they go.

If you want people to follow your rule, be honest and polite. Be yourself and be good to others. Yes, we all can do this.

Many people around the world take leadership positions because they like money, fame, and power, but they have nothing to show for it. When they run campaigns, they seem to champion the causes of the people; however, after the people have voted them into power, these leaders seek their own interests and forget about the people.

Instead of displaying good leadership, they display greed and abuse of power. They abandon the good virtues of leadership and become corrupt and wicked.

Jesus, speaking to his disciples about leadership, said this:

[85]*You know that the rulers of the Gentiles lord it over them, and their high officials exercise authority over them. Not so with you. Instead, whoever wants to become great among you must be your servant.* [Matthew 20:25-26]

Ouch! What a block to the ego! Jesus understood that leaders are elected by the people and should work for the people, not the other way around.

He warned his disciples that the power and authority he gave them should not be used to boss people around. Instead, if they wanted to remain in leadership positions, they had to serve the people.

Because leadership serves the best interests of the people, every leadership role is effective only to the extent to which it serves the people. Leadership is not for the leader's self-gratification and personal aggrandizement.

The position is not your cocoa farm; no, it is not your grandpa's business that you inherited. You are put there for a time to serve the people; if you serve correctly, the people will keep you there. You should serve the people.

I pray that leaders in Africa will hear this message. I pray that leaders in Latin America will hear this message. I pray that people in the Middle East will hear this message. This message is important for the people of Russia, Germany, Great Britain, and the great United States of America.

Advanced Western countries have a way of doing bad things secretly and raining damaging effects on businesses, middle-class people, and poor people, even in the midst of plenty. We all must serve the people.

Job recognized God in the world when he said,

[86]*Dominion and awe belong to God; he establishes order in the heights of heaven.* [Job 25:2]

When we understand that all we have comes from God, we will recognize the issue of accountability. God gave us his world to tend and care for; he gave us people and things to rule.

Understanding this will help us be mindful about the ways in which we lead and exercise our dominion. We cannot simply lead any possible way; we must lead correctly.

Good leadership is so important; God assured us of this when he made people and animals fear those who approached as leaders.

A leader's gender, size, and age do not matter; when a good leader approaches, everyone gets into place. It is God who gave leaders that spirit; if he did not do so, our leadership would not be duly respected.

Leaders must be recognized; that is why the writer of Genesis said,

[87]*The fear and dread of you will fall on all the beasts of the earth, and on all the birds in the sky, on every creature that moves along the ground, and on all the fish in the sea; they are given into your hands.* [Genesis 9:2]

All this happens because we are leaders. God has called us not only to lead, but to lead with consciousness, accountability, and vision.

When people honor and respect us because of our positions, we must humble ourselves and show them kindness in return. It is very important that we reciprocate the honor.

Serve people beyond their expectation and you will leave behind a legacy.

Be the leader that sets the gold standard, a legend whom people will talk about for years to come. In the eyes of God, you are that special; so let it be in your life.

As leaders with dominion, we must perform beyond the call of duty. We must serve the people, act in their behalf above and beyond what the books require. When we abandon the limitations of our leadership duties and go to the place of sacrifice, we are setting a gold standard. The truth is that people who succeed in life do not follow small rules of operation that limit their abilities.

They know the rules and follow them, but they become people who do extra things so that the people or organization can move to the next level and beat the competition. They do not sit back and wait to be told what to do. They have brains to think and plan for the best interests of the people and organizations they work for.

Leaders who do this are not mere leaders; their leadership becomes magnetic and contagious. These are the types of people to whom, because of their good governance, others come and voluntarily declare their loyalty.

They demonstrate a high class of leadership that others want to emulate. They automatically become leaders of leaders because, when administrating over their dominion, they rely on integrity, love, and care. They pay the price for good governance. In the Bible, Daniel said of God:

[88]*In your hands he has placed all mankind and the beasts of the field and the birds in the sky. Wherever they live, he has made you ruler over them all. You are that head of gold.* [Daniel 2:38]

God has made us the head of gold; that is why we must set the gold standard. What is the gold standard? It is the highest mark of achievement in life's disciplines. It is a place of performance that others use to set the mark of success in various areas of life and work.

We are Born to Take Charge. For unto us God has said, "Be Fruitful, Multiply, Fill the Earth, Subdue it, and have Dominion." God has given us this five-fold charge that he expects us to accomplish.

God knows that we are capable of fulfilling our purposes in life. God knows that we can reach our destinies in life. However, we cannot do it without knowing how to get there.

First of all, we must understand that we are Born to Take Charge. We must truly understand our place in the world if we are to tend and care for the creation of God.

We must understand that God has given us power and authority over the fowls of the air, the beasts of the land, and the fish in the waters. Simply put, God has given us authority over land, air, and water.

As individuals, we have personal goals that form part of God's sovereign agenda for this world. God has given us everything we need to succeed.

Let us not sit back as though we are incompetent in any way; we have what it takes to do the job. If we are not sure about something, we can ask the Master to show us the way; he is always around and willing to intervene should we ask him.

Note, though, that just because God has put things in our charge and has given us will and choice, through our decisions we can either recognize and invite him in, or go alone without him. It is all up to us.

Now let us look back for a moment to ponder a simple question; this will be a personal thing. How did you get here? I am talking about where you are now. What have you done with your life so far? I know you are ready to explain, but wait until you consider the following.

Do you really think that you have done much with your life, with all the people and things that God gave you, including the places to which you have been exposed? Are you living your life to the fullest?

Now tell me, what is your answer? God is watching to see whether you will answer the questions with honesty. This is simple. We must stop blaming others for everything that happened to us, and we must find a way to channel our lives.

We must stop living in the past; we must stop living empty words and start taking meaningful steps toward leading our lives along the right path.

Again, let me remind you: you are not a looser; stop thinking like one. You are not a 'drop-out'; you are not worthless. You are worth something. You are not a "nobody." God has made you somebody. You are beautifully and wonderfully made; you are a unique person.

Your DNA, fingerprints, and teeth are unique, totally different from those of everyone else in the whole wide world. So why do you go around with your head and shoulders down as though life has no meaning? Wake up! Wake up! It is time to do something.

It was because of you that God said to the prophet Isaiah:

[89]*Arise, shine, for your light has come, and the glory of the Lord rises upon you.* [Isaiah 60:1]

God made you a leader, an overseer, and a steward of his wonderful creation, yet you are going around like a flower tossed about by the wind. You are supposed to be in control.

Some of you have been abused so frequently that you created a bond with the abuser, attached yourself to him or her, lied and denied the abuse, all to protect the offender. You have lowered your own value so much; that is not good at all. It is because of you that Prophet Isaiah said, "Arise and shine." It is your time.

To the woman with no hope because men have used and dumped her: I say Arise.

To the man with no job and no education who is hopeless: unto you I say Arise.

To the community leader with no one to help: Do not give up because help is on the way; you must Arise and Shine.

To the pastor who stands strong in the Word of God while things are falling apart: God sees your faithfulness; do not lose heart. The Glory of the Lord rises upon you. You have been faithful in the midst of little things; because of that, God will make you ruler of bigger things.

To all the faint-hearted people out there, to those who are depressed, to those who want to commit suicide because they think life is hard and meaningless, I say to you: Arise and Shine, for your Light has come.

I am Yahweh but I am also Elohim. I know the end in the beginning. I make a way out of no way. Ask Moses, ask Joshua. Ask the Jews during the Holocaust. Go to West Africa and ask the people in Liberia and Sierra Leone how I did it.

To the soldiers out there on the frontlines: you know how I helped you narrowly escape death. I saved your men. I kept you for a purpose. I say to you: Arise and Shine.

To the men out there who have done it and done it and done it and now want to settle down but cannot find peace: do not lose heart. The women and children you hurt while taking part in your nonsense are mine, but I can forgive you.

Do not be in a hurry to succeed and leave me behind; you need me. I will take you to the potter's house, where I remake broken clay. I will break and mold you into something more wonderful, something desirable. Your life will never be the same, but you must wait.

To the people who do not know me or who do not want to know me: I AM. Ask me, try me, and see how I will do.

I told Malachi to tell Israel to test me with tithes and offerings and to see how I responded. Today, many people who follow me carry my name, yet live in shame, poverty, and sickness. They bring shame to my good name because they ignore my word about giving.

People who do not know me are afraid of what they will learn about me. They are afraid to agree that I am He who made them what they are. I give, I take; sometimes I confuse the wise and make the simple wise. I AM.

If you know an atheist friend or an unbelieving friend, tell them that I want to visit with them. I want to give them a life beyond what they know. I am the giver of good things beyond imagination. I made man and everything he knows. I let him know because I am the Omniscient God.

Because I AM, I will begin to show myself more often to man in his knowledge; this will confuse some and affirm others. I AM.

I want you to know—I mean you who are reading this book—that I have a plan for you. I will work with you. But I want you to do yourself a favor and ask me just one thing.

Say unto me: God, Fix_Me_Up. Say it. Say it like you really mean it from your heart and I will visit with you throughout the next few days to prove that I AM. I want something better for you. What I will do with you is not just for you, but for the benefit of the people out there. Oh yes, I know not all of you have followers now. You see, that's the problem; people have been waiting for you to come alive and shine.

Enjoy your life, but do not forget that I, who gives, takes away. Live graciously. Why don't you bow your head now and talk to me. Say a few words of prayer. I am waiting. Good day.

I AM.

PART FIVE:
Pray Hard and Work Hard

Life is an arena in which performance is required and actually demanded. We are tossed off stage if we do not perform accordingly. The crowds applaud and ask for more if we give them the performance they expect.

Because life can be difficult, we must work hard and pray hard to succeed. There is no food for the lazy man. You and I cannot become liabilities for others. If people put in time and effort to get where they are, we should do our part and not become mere beggars. We must become people who can give something back to society.

Many people are counting on us. Our parents, school teachers, family, friends, community, and the world at large are seeking people who will make a difference. Those who work hard and go beyond the normal tides of success are people we hail as heroes and celebrities.

You are a hero. I am a hero. We are celebrities in our own right; let us make others see what we are capable of. The world has not seen us the way we must be seen. Let us work hard to reveal ourselves. For this reason, we must Work Hard and Pray Hard.

Chapter 16: Faith - The God Factor

In this world that can be so inconsiderate to low performers and non-performers, we are all at stake. We must do something or lose something. That is why we all must Pray Hard and Work Hard. It is true that nothing is for nothing and that nothing comes easy.

All of us have faith. Whether our faith is in God, people, or things, we all have a faith that we express every day. For example, we take letters and packages to the post office, expressing our faith that with the fee we pay, our letters or packages will reach their desired destinations on time. We do this even though we do not know the clerks or mail carriers. We give our things to total strangers and expect them to work diligently for us. We apply faith.

I bring up the issue of faith because, in our daily interactions with people, we express faith and belief. I want us to increase our faith and belief in the things that matter most. We should ask God to help us. We should initiate some activity to achieve our goals. We must work with other people and trust that they will play their part in helping us to reach our goals.

In addition, we must place a high premium on ourselves. We must have self-esteem and exhibit the will of a winner. Nobody wants to invest in a loser, especially a constant loser. To achieve the best results, we must apply faith to our work. It is good to work, but when we do not believe in our work, we get weary and stop pressing forward. It is the faith we have in our own efforts, coupled with contributions from others, that help us reach our goals.

Thus, when it comes to work, faith is very important. We must be convinced that with our work and the necessary daily adjustments we make, our goals are not far off.

There are things we do well that do not require much faith and work. Such things are easy for us to handle; we can pick the time and place to do them without a problem. Yet sometimes, after we have worked so hard, things do not seem to fall into place. To this end, I encourage everyone to apply faith and prayer. Why faith and prayer?

Faith helps us maintain the belief that our hard work will succeed; prayer seals the deal by assuring us that we will get our answer through divine intervention. Prayer connects the dots and makes things happen behind the scenes. It intercedes on our behalf so that things will work out according to plan; they all work well together.

The writer of the book of Deuteronomy talks about God in this way. He said,

[90]*He is the Rock, his works are perfect, and all his ways are just. A faithful God who does no wrong, upright and just is he. The works are God are perfect and he is faithful.* [Deuteronomy 32:4]

How does this apply to us? When our work is not complete or appealing, the God of perfection takes our imperfect work and uses it to bless us and help us succeed in life.

He adds the finishing touches to our work. Our limitations in performance do not stop him from helping us. If God wants perfect work from perfect people, then most of us—if not all of us—are at the losing end because we are not perfect. However, God is faithful; when he promised to take care of us, he meant what he said.

Chapter 17: Work - The Human Factor

King David of Israel said of God,

⁹¹The works of his hands are faithful and just; all his precepts are trustworthy. [Psalm 111:6]

God is faithful; God is worthy. He is faithful to us as his children. He is worthy of our trust in him. He does not fail us. He is worthy of our service and praise.

The psalmist said of the Lord,

⁹²All your works praise you, Lord; your faithful people extol you. [Psalm 145:10]

The handiwork of God is breathtaking. Just watch the night sky or see images from deep space, deep sea, or deep earth; you will marvel at how great the Lord is.

God is good; he wants the works of our hands to be good as well. He wants us to create a signature series that will be in demand. He does not desire for us to offer things that no one wants. God wants us to put our minds and hearts into our work.

As God has worked to give us the cosmos, and has given us the charge to care for and tend it, he expects us to do some work here and to do it well.

When it comes to work, God expects us to bring something to the table. He does not expect us to follow dogmas.

God has given us the most powerful machine ever known—the human brain—and he expects us to use it. With the proper administration of our brains, we can imagine, think, dream, and create things.

We can employ our thoughts to bring us creativity and innovation that powers our visions and aspirations for life. The human mind is very powerful. Do not waste yours.

If something new must be done, it is done. Why not you? New inventions emerge daily; technology is improving our world.

You can be one of the young or old minds that are restless until they produce something or improve on something. Why not you? I want you to understand that you are one of a kind; you must do what you can to prove what you are capable of.

It is not a good thing to sit back with that recipe or that new computer, military, or arts-and-entertainment idea as though you know nothing. Put together whatever you have and bring it to the table.

The world is waiting for your idea and for your hard work. You must perform. Do not worry about what stage to use. Create your own stage, a new type of stage that will elevate your dreams and visions.

The Apostle Paul said that,

[93]*For we maintain that a person is justified by faith apart from the works of the law.* [Romans 3:28]

In talking about dogmatism in the law without proper application of faith, Paul makes this remarkable statement that our faith has a way of justifying our work. When the reason for our work is expressed by our faith, then faith justifies our work. I like that. We cannot simply answer "yes sir" or "yes ma'am" without using our brains. We have leverage and we should use it with wisdom.

You can surprise your spouse, kids, friends, and boss with something new and innovative. You can do something on our own without their directive. It speaks to your maturity and says that you can be trusted with little or no supervision.

Let me be quick to interject something here; before we all start jumping in and doing things, please understand this. As we take a leap of faith in our work and break from our daily routines, we must be mindful. Just as faith without work is dead, so it is that work without faith is boring and dead.

To reach our goal, we must balance work and faith. James, the brother of Jesus, said,

[94]*What good is it, my brothers and sisters, if someone claims to have faith but has no deeds? But someone will say, "You have faith; I have deeds." Show me your faith without deeds, and I will show you my faith by my deeds. You foolish person, do you want evidence that*

faith without deeds is useless? As the body without the spirit is dead, so faith without deeds is dead. [James 2:14, 18, 20, 26]

To put this in perspective, think about it as follows,

Faith says I believe, so I do—work; work shows that I believe, so I apply action—faith.

I understand that it is good to start from somewhere; we all do, but staying too long in any one place will bring problems.

Doing the same thing over and over is boring, unwanted repetition; it stalls creativity and kills progress. We all have some platform on which to perform; I think we should use it properly.

We must learn to think outside of the box and step into the world of exploration and adventure. To broaden your horizon, perhaps you need to take a walk, a drive, or a flight to a new environment, or hang out with new people.

I do not understand how some people today are very smart and creative but do not display their talents and skills because they are waiting for somebody to give them the "go-ahead" signal. They become like dead car batteries that need a jumpstart. Why?

You have a brain; I have a brain. In Liberia we say, "Use your head." Why must we wait for somebody to use their brains before we can use our own? Would you not get angry if someone told you that you have no brains? A plan works only when someone jumpstarts it.

Life is an arena of performance. You either perform well and get applause, get thrown off stage for a poor performance, or get stoned for non-performance. Therefore, we must do something with what we have and make it count.

It is that "something" inside of us that will inspire people to talk, see, touch, and invest.

By all means, we must be ready to do what is expected of us and to transcend the realm of surprises. You are not a loser; stop acting like one.

There are more than six billion people (and counting) in the world today. Those who are in the headlines for their successes are those who have used their brains. What about you, my dear? As you still waiting for a command before you use your head? Or will you rise up, put yourself together, and begin to use your head?

I am using my head. I had to, as too many thoughts were bubbling inside it. I could no longer contain them so I had to put them together and do something. This book is just one of the things that I am doing. I am working. Go work!

Chapter 18: Prayer Changes Things

At times our problem is not that we do not do something, but that we overly do things. When we work harder than necessary, we go beyond the acquisition of perfection to a place of overachievement.

When this happens, we usually miss the mark even though we can do the thing we set out to do. We must be precise. We cannot poorly perform or do nothing.

When we struggle with poor self-esteem, or when we wait for a "go" command before we act, or when we simply do nothing, something is telling us that it is time to pray.

A little help from heaven will carry us a long way in our journey to performance. If our problem is that we overshoot and keep missing the mark, we must ask God to help us—perhaps by providing someone to train us—so that we can aim better.

Whenever we want something, we must go for it. There was a troubled woman named Hannah. She was bereft of a child due to infertility. She took matter into her own hands and sought the Lord in prayer.

Today when many people take matters into their own hands, things go terribly wrong. However, Hannah took positive steps to avoid reproach.

Even though the priest accused her of drunkenness, she did not relent in her prayers; in the end, she bore a son who became a prophet and leader of Israel.

Prophet Samuel, Hannah's miracle son, anointed Saul and David as kings over Israel. Hannah's prayers did not just give her a son; they gave her a proud son who became the leader of the nation of Israel and a powerful prophet. What can your work and prayers do?

Here is the account,

[95]There was a certain man from Ramathaim, a Zuphite from the hill country of Ephraim, whose name was Elkanah son of Jeroham, the son of Elihu, the son of Tohu, the son of Zuph, an Ephraimite. He had two wives; one was called Hannah and the other Peninnah. Peninnah had children, but Hannah had none.

Year after year this man went up from his town to worship and sacrifice to the Lord Almighty at Shiloh, where Hophni and Phinehas, the two sons of Eli were priests of the Lord. Whenever the day came for Elkanah to sacrifice, he would give portions of the meat to his wife Peninnah and to all her sons and daughters. But to Hannah he gave a double portion because he loved her, and the Lord had closed her womb. Because the Lord had closed Hannah's womb, her rival kept provoking her in order to irritate her. This went on year after year.

Whenever Hannah went up to the house of the Lord, her rival provoked her till she wept and would not eat. Her husband Elkanah would say to her, "Hannah, why are you weeping? Why don't you eat? Why are you downhearted? Don't I mean more to you than ten sons?"

Once when they had finished eating and drinking in Shiloh, Hannah stood up. Now Eli the priest was sitting on his chair by the doorpost of the Lord's house. In her deep anguish Hannah prayed to the Lord, weeping bitterly. And she made a vow, saying, "Lord Almighty, if you will only look on your servant's misery and remember me, and not forget your servant but give her a son, then I will give him to the Lord for all the days of his life, and no razor will ever be used on his head."

As she kept on praying to the Lord, Eli observed her mouth. Hannah was praying in her heart, and her lips were moving but her voice was not heard. Eli thought she was drunk and said to her, "How long are you going to stay drunk?

Put away your wine." "Not so, my lord," Hannah replied, "I am a woman who is deeply troubled. I have not been drinking wine or beer; I was pouring out my soul to the Lord. Do not take your servant for a wicked woman; I have been praying here out of my great anguish and grief."

Eli answered, "Go in peace, and may the God of Israel grant you what you have asked of him." She said, "May your servant find favor in your eyes." Then she went her way and ate something, and her face was no longer downcast.

Early the next morning they arose and worshiped before the Lord and then went back to their home at Ramah. Elkanah made love to his wife Hannah, and the Lord remembered her. So in the course of time Hannah became pregnant and gave birth to a son. She named him Samuel, saying, "Because I asked the Lord for him." [I Samuel 1:1-20]

What a touching story! Hannah did it. She employed faith and work to get her answer. In faith she said, "I will go to the temple to pray." In work, she did not talk or blame others, but instead went to the temple and prayed seriously until the priest noticed her.

Even though the priest wrongly accused her, she took the time to correct him because he carried the power of God that was necessary to produce her miracle. Sometimes pastors and other leaders can get things wrong because they are human; they do not pray or think things through before responding to us. They make mistakes.

When this happens, like Hannah, let us correct them gracefully because they have the anointing and leadership to settle our matter. Acting rude or calling them bad names behind their backs are bad ideas.

In your time of struggle, do not be harsh and aggressive to those who do not understand your plight; take the time to correct them.

In your time of struggle, pray until the man or woman of God notices you. This person can speak divine utterances over your life and achieve your miracle. Be nice to people. Perhaps they will be part of the solution.

Hannah's consistent prayers and gentle response to the priest inspired the priest to make divine declarations over her life, thus producing her miracle. According to the word from the man of God, the priest, in due time Hannah conceived a son.

I love this story because it does not say that we should sit back and expect others to do everything for us; no, we must take initiative. Some people carry around grudges and blame others all day long instead of fighting their own fights. This is bad and a terrible waste of time. Let us be like Hannah and fight for what we want in life by applying faith, prayer, and work.

I do not understand why so many Christians today do not know how to pray—and I mean, really pray. Some of them know how to pray, but they do not; they would rather ask other people to pray for them.

Sometimes it is like they are buying prayer. They do not pray at all because they have paid other people to pray for them. If you know anybody like that, please send them to me. I need the cash!

Please do not criticize me. I know that at times we must ask others to pray for us; but as they pray, we too must pray. It should be a prayer of agreement. They are there to support our efforts. We should not wander off to eat, party, or do other things just because we "sowed seeds" and someone is praying for us.

On the contrary, our need for answers and miracles should draw us closer to God. It should help us communicate with him more. God is not interested simply in answering our prayers; he wants to build us into great men and women of faith who can withstand the enemy's attacks.

In prayer, people communicate with God. Prayer is not always about asking for things. We need communication with God, just as we need to talk with family and friends daily.

Meanwhile, when it comes to times of trouble, many people are not able to pray. Keep in mind that even Jesus Christ prayed always and taught his disciples to pray as well.

Today, many Christians pray only on Sundays when they should be praying every day. I want to encourage all of us to pray. Christians must pray and pray always. If Jesus Christ prayed alone, why do we wait for Sundays? The gospel writer Matthew tells us that Jesus prayed alone.

[96]Immediately Jesus made the disciples get into the boat and go on ahead of him to the other side, while he dismissed the crowd. After he had dismissed them, he went up on a mountainside by himself to pray. Later that night, he was there alone. [Matthew 14:23]

It is good to pray corporately as believers at church, but church services are only a few hours long. We need to pray more.

Jesus always prayed by himself. Let us learn from our Master and pray alone. I have come to understand that at some times we must really pray by ourselves.

During such times, I believe God wants to commune with us as his children. Therefore, other people do not have to be there. God wants to talk heart-to-heart with us. In such times as these, we all must pray more.

We must pray by ourselves, pray as family, pray in groups, and pray at church. Because of the importance of prayer, Jesus Christ taught his disciples how to pray when he said:

⁹⁷This, then, is how you should pray:

"'Our Father in heaven, hallowed be your name, your kingdom come, your will be done, on earth as it is in heaven. Give us today our daily bread. And forgive us our debts, as we also have forgiven our debtors. And lead us not into temptation, but deliver us from the evil one.'

For if you forgive other people when they sin against you, your heavenly Father will also forgive you. But if you do not forgive others their sins, your Father will not forgive your sins." [Matthew 6:9-15]

When praying, it is important to recognize that we have a father. He is in heaven watching over us. Our father has a kingdom and we should do his will. He cares and provides for us in every dimension.

We can ask for our needs; I know that many of us are very good at praying this type of prayer. Sometimes it seems as though the only times we pray are when we want something. I wonder what God thinks of us when we do this. It is not good at all.

I think it makes us look bad. It shows that we do not care about God; we just want things.

Jesus taught his disciples to pray, to ask God for forgiveness of our sins, transgressions, and debts. Interestingly, Jesus also says that we must partake of the forgiveness process ourselves.

This means that, just as God forgives us, we must forgive others. In the negative sense, it means that we agree that God should not forgive us if we do not forgive those who have offended us.

This is a serious matter. We need to pray honestly that we will do what the father wants; otherwise, when we are unwilling to forgive, we bring problems upon ourselves.

We are reminded that evil is in this world and that it can tempt us; however, God helps us in the midst of temptation and delivers us from all evil. Temptations are real; they assail us every day. People who do not like us tempt us; friends and family have a way of tempting us, too.

When we know the people who tempt us, the pain can be heavy because we expect that they will be there for us; that they will not push us off balance into something that will destroy us.

Jesus Christ makes it clear that we must forgive others as God forgives us. Our refusal or unwillingness to forgive could prevent us from receiving forgiveness. Forgiveness is reciprocal.

When we are kind enough to forgive those who wrong us, even though we believe that they do not deserve forgiveness, other people will find it easier to forgive us for our own errors.

True forgiveness brings healing and reunion. However, if the offender does not want to come forth and associate with you, or if the offender still does things to undermine you, you must do everything you can to stay clear of him or her. If you must interact with the offender, be vigilant and order your steps carefully.

We may think that others do not deserve our forgiveness, and we might be right. Yet when we forgive them, we free ourselves from a heavy load. By forgiving, we do ourselves a favor because we relieve ourselves of the heaviness we carry every time we see or remember the person. If you struggle with this, please ask God to help you in prayer.

I want to spend a little more time talking about the power of prayer. Prayer can do many things for us and for the world. Prayer can even affect nature; Moses, Joshua, Elijah, Elisha, and many others have done it. Prayer can affect the weather. Prayer can affect plants and animals. Prayer can change people.

Many people often think about prayer in the context of healing and deliverance, but I want to tell you that prayer does a lot more to touch heaven and make the impossible possible.

[98]*Early in the morning, as Jesus was on his way back to the city, he was hungry. Seeing a fig tree by the road, he went up to it but found nothing on it except leaves. Then he said to it, "May you never bear fruit again!" Immediately the tree withered.*

When the disciples saw this, they were amazed. "How did the fig tree wither so quickly?" they asked. Jesus replied, "Truly I tell you, if you have faith and do not doubt, not only can you do what was done to the fig tree, but also you can say to this mountain, 'Go, throw yourself into the sea,' and it will be done." [Matthew 21:18-21]

Wow, prayer killed the tree that looked good but did not bear any fruit. Jesus went on to say that if we believe and do not doubt in our prayers, we can command great things like mountains out of our way. Let me ask you this: what is the mountain in your way today? Pray it away.

Why not command it in the name of Jesus with prayer and take appropriate steps for your miracle? I think we should all do that. Some problems do not want to go away, but prayer can make a difference.

We must use our power of prayer and command things to get out of our way. What is giving you a hard time today? Why not kill it in prayer? Jesus did it; you can do it, too.

There is record of a man in Israel named Prophet Elijah who commanded drought for three and a half years; then, he called rain to fall at his word. This same man brought down fire from heaven to burn an altar during the reign of King Ahaz, whose wife was Jezebel. This is the story.

[99]At the time of sacrifice, the prophet Elijah stepped forward and prayed: "Lord, the God of Abraham, Isaac and Israel, let it be known today that you are God in Israel and that I am your servant and have done all these things at your command.

Answer me, LORD, answer me, so these people will know that you, LORD, are God, and that you are turning their hearts back again."

Then the fire of the LORD fell and burned up the sacrifice, the wood, the stones and the soil, and also licked up the water in the trench. When all the people saw this, they fell prostrate and cried,

"The LORD—he is God! The LORD—he is God!"

At the time of sacrifice, the prophet Elijah stepped forward and prayed: "LORD, the God of Abraham, Isaac and Israel, let it be known today that you are God in Israel and that I am your servant and have done all these things at your command.

Answer me, LORD, answer me, so these people will know that you, LORD, are God, and that you are turning their hearts back again."

Then the fire of the LORD fell and burned up the sacrifice, the wood, the stones and the soil, and also licked up the water in the trench. When all the people saw this, they fell prostrate and cried, "The LORD—he is God! The LORD—he is God!" [I Kings 18:36-39]

When we pray, the expressed power of God manifests in us to do the impossible, the unthinkable, and the unbelievable. Prayer truly has power.

A young army general named Joshua, who was Moses's aide, stopped the sun so that he could finish a battle. Joshua prayed for God to stop the sun and the sun stopped.

The Bible says,

[100] *So the sun stood still, and the moon stopped, till the nation avenged itself on its enemies, as it is written in the Book of Jashar. The sun stopped in the middle of the sky and delayed going down about a full day.* [Joshua 10:13]

Wow, every time we pray, something happens. God can perform wonders when we pray. What can your prayers do?

To all the husbands and wives who suffer from infertility, I want to encourage you to do like Isaac and pray.

I know it is disconcerting to see abortion advocates calling young babies fetuses so that they can reduce their moral guilt about killing our young. Interestingly, fetuses grow and turn into real humans like you and me.

Today in third-world countries like those in West Africa, women are abused both verbally and physically because of infertility. I want to encourage couples and their families to pray and seek medical attention when have a problem of childlessness.

The Bible states that,

[101] *Isaac prayed to the Lord on behalf of his wife, because she was childless. The Lord answered his prayer, and his wife Rebekah became pregnant. Isaac prayed for his wife and God answered him.* [Genesis 25:21]

The wife feels secure when the man takes the time to love and support her in every way. The woman is moved when she sees the man pray for her. It goes beyond romance to deep love.

I want to encourage men to be there for their women and to pray for them. When you find a wife, it is a good thing; the woman is part of you and you are part of her. Let her mourning and joy be equally shared. Do not be an uncaring, selfish partner who thinks only about yourself.

We must love our wives whether or not they give us babies. I also want to encourage women to value the efforts that men put in during this sensitive time. As the women suffer, the men also bear the pains; the key is to be there for each other no matter what.

Let us now turn our attention to the church. The church, the sanctuary of God, is supposed to be the epicenter of prayer. Do not get me wrong; a church building is not the only place to pray, but it is a place set aside for the sole purpose of prayer, worship, fellowship, and ministry.

If the building is set aside for the purpose of worship, it should maintain a certain presence of God. This is why church buildings are usually dedicated to the service of God in prayer.

The church building is the primary place we congregate to pray. It is a place where problems receive solutions. It is no surprise that Jesus said,

[102]*My house will be called "a house of prayer," but you are making it "a den of robbers."* [Matthew 21:13]

Sadly, today many churches are not prayer centers, but rather business centers for crooked pastors. Instead of teaching members how to pray, these pastors consider themselves gurus whom parishioners must consult and pay.

Jesus Christ taught his disciples to pray. We must teach the people of the church to pray and not to make a profit off their parishioners. I have been to a few such churches.

Some churches carry a certain presence of God because their parishioners pray. When you enter such churches, you know that the Lord is there. Other churches look good and are well decorated, but do not have the presence of God. Every church should carry an evident presence of God.

Sometimes it seems as though we can measure the capacity of God's power to some extent because of our sensitivity to the Spirit of God. The level or magnitude of prayers creates an atmosphere conducive to worship.

When the church prays, even the building and its surroundings can be anointed; that is how it should be. Jesus said that the church should be called a "house of prayer" and not a "den of robbers." It is my prayer that the Lord will help the modern church discover the value of prayer.

The church should pray because prayer has power; prayer changes things. Prayer inflicts casualties in the camp of the devil—our principal enemy. Pray because prayer heals. Prayer delivers. Prayer opens and closes doors. Prayer can make a way out of no way. Prayer restores and prayer promotes.

Because of the solemnity of prayer and the immensity of our problems Jesus says,

[103]*If you believe, you will receive whatever you ask for in prayer.* [Matthew 21:22]

Prayer takes faith and work. In faith, we believe that God will answer us; in work we take part in the act of prayer and other undertakings as God leads us. When it comes to deliverance from demonic oppression, Jesus said,

[104]*This kind can come out only by prayer and fasting.* [Mark 9:29]

When we pray serious and fervent prayers, God responds to us. When demons infest the lives of people and inflict them with all kinds of evil things, only serious prayer will cast them out.

In deliverance we must have faith and do serious prayer. We must listen to the leadership of the Holy Spirit and pray with faith; if we do, the Lord will deliver the oppressed.

When you talk to people who believe in the power of prayer and who really pray, you will hear many wonderful stories about how God works miracles.

All Christians must take prayer seriously. Christians are called to pray for the nation and its leaders. We are called to pray for our families and friends whether or not they believe in God. We must pray every day for ourselves and for the leadership of God in our lives.

We should not limit our prayers to petitions and supplications. The next time you call to heaven, do not let it not be because you want something; we can call just to talk to God as father.

We can talk to him and express our love and adoration for him. We can call just to give him heartfelt worship. I love to pray for anything and all things, but when I pray just to worship, I reach my highest state of connectedness to God.

There is something wonderful about prayer and worship. May God help all of us discover the proper application of faith, prayer, and work; our lives depend on it.

If the prayers of Moses opened the Red Sea and Israel crossed on dry land, if the prayers of Joshua stopped the sun, if the prayers of Elijah stopped the rain, then caused it to return, then brought down fire, we must all pray. And if the prayers of Elijah and Elisha opened the Jordan River, if the prayers of Daniel made hungry lions become his friends, and if the quick prayers of Shadrach, Meshach, and Abednego stopped the fire from burning them, then prayer should be an essential part of our lives.

Now let me ask you few simple questions. What can your prayers and my prayers do? What can your faith and mine, coupled with proper work, do?

What about you and me today? If the prayers of ordinary people and leaders of yesterday changed things, and if prayer still works, what can our prayers do today?

The devil is afraid of the power in our prayers of faith and divine declarations. Because of this, he makes many Christians, and even pastors, not pray. No prayer actually means no power; when there is no power, the devil can really play with your life!

Today I challenge you to pray, have faith, and declare the word. Stop paying people to pray for you when you can ask God to teach you how to pray.

When we pray, things change. I challenge you to have faith, pray, and work; if you do, God will help you. Remember, you are nothing less than a winner because you were Born to Take Charge. In all you do, please remember to always pray. God bless you, my dear friend.

PART SIX:
WAIT!

Wait!

Joseph waited 13 years. From the dungeons he became the prime minister of Egypt in one day.

Abraham waited 25 years. It took that long for the birth of his promised son. Even though he made some terrible mistakes, he got his son, Isaac.

Moses waited 40 years. While defending helpless Israelites suffering in captivity and performing heavy labor in Egypt, he killed a man and fled for his life in Median. It took forty years before he had the burning bush experience in which God called on him to tell Pharaoh to let Israel go.

And Jesus waited 30 years! Imagine this one. Our Lord and savior Jesus had to wait 30 years before he began his public ministry.

So why are you rushing? Please do not die before your time. Wait. Your time will come. It is disconcerting to tell someone to wait when all of life is moving so fast and everyone wants to get ahead.

I know how impatient we are nowadays. We are always in a hurry. We live in a fast-paced society. Most of us drive above the speed limit, run red lights, and jump ahead of people in line. We do not like to wait. Why?

We are told to "think it and claim it," "move forward," and "wake up your inner person." All of these motivational themes are good, but when we apply them without waiting for an opportune time, disaster can result.

We must all learn the art of waiting. To wait does not mean that we are inadequate in any way; it is a virtue we need in life, especially if we want to succeed. It is quite important to wait; we should not rush into everything. We must learn to wait.

Join me in this chapter as we discuss this very important theme. Wait!

- Waiting is Not Doing Nothing
- Waiting Prepares Us
- Waiting Gives Us Knowledge
- Waiting Instills Character
- Waiting Brings Rewards

Chapter 19: Waiting Is Not Doing Nothing

There is a sharp difference between waiting and doing nothing. There are people who do not initiate any activities to move forward in life. They just lie around, eat, sleep, and sometimes blame others for their problems. They expect others to take care of them. They are simply liabilities.

In our time of waiting, we must get busy doing something useful.

Time is too precious a commodity to waste.

For all of us who are Christians, the Bible says a lot about patience and waiting. There is nothing that says sit down, lie down, eat all day, sleep all night, and do nothing. In our time of waiting, we must get busy doing something.

The Apostle Paul, writing to the church in Rome, said,

[105] *But if we hope for what we do not see, we eagerly wait for it with perseverance.* [Romans 8:25]

In waiting, we hope for things that should be that are not yet. We should wait eagerly, with patience and anticipation. We must do something as we wait. As we wait for our time in life, we should not forget about all the things God has done for us. Sometimes in our time of waiting, we become weary and forget that the same God who helped us yesterday is the same God today and forever.

When people get caught up in their problems or their desire for success,

[106] *They soon forgot His works; they did not wait for his counsel.* [Psalm 106:13]

We should not forget God during our times of distress or when we strive for success. It is not a time to sit back and do nothing; instead, each day, when we wake up in the morning, let each of us say in a personal way,

¹⁰⁷My soul, wait silently for God alone, for my expectation is from Him. [Psalm 62:5]

As we wait for God to give us the desires of our hearts, we cannot sit around without doing anything.

¹⁰⁸For we through the Spirit eagerly wait for hope of righteousness by faith. [Galatians 5:5]

It is interesting to know that,

Intelligent people educate themselves; poor people entertain themselves.

One would think that it is the rich and intelligent folks who sit back and do nothing except play poker, watch videos or sports, and sip wine in ballrooms. No, not at all.

Sadly, it is quite the opposite. Even though the rich and powerful know how to have fun—and they do that quite well—they do not let fun interfere with business. They know when to work and when to play.

Even though they are rich and have things and people at their command, they are usually the hardest working people around. They work and do their share of the job.

It hurts to know that many times it is the poor and suffering masses who do not want to work. They do not want to take the time to learn anything. They do not want to wait for anything. Some of them are busy doing nothing. They roam around aimlessly like waves of the sea tossed by the winds.

Many of them think that things happen by magic or miracle. They would rather go on with whatever they are doing than take the time to wait and learn something that will benefit them.

Though life demands that we do something, we must not go rushing into things without preparing ourselves. As we wait for our time, we must not sit back and do nothing.

During our time to wait, we must prepare and acquire knowledge and character so we can reap the rewards that patient people receive.

Chapter 20: Waiting Prepares Us

It is funny how many people rush into things without proper preparation. When we rush into things without preparing, we make rash decisions about who to connect with and how things should be. We leave out important details.

The Bible encourages us to,

[109]*Wait on the Lord; be of good courage, and He shall strengthen your heart; Wait, I say, on the Lord!* [Psalm 27:14]

Waiting on God gives us strength, which is something we all need to face the challenges of life. Wait helps us gain strength in our hearts; most of us are not strong enough.

There are many things in life we must wait for; we must prepare for them before we can really enjoy them. It is the same way we must respond to our place in this world. We must wait for our time. We must prepare for it before it passes, before we realize that it already arrived.

James, the brother of Jesus, reminded the church to be patient as we wait on the Lord.

[110]*Therefore be patient, brethren, until the coming of the Lord. See how the farmer waits for the precious fruit of the earth, waiting patiently for it until it receives the early and latter rain.* [James 5:7]

If we consider life valuable, we must value our time. We must wait patiently and prepare for the opportunities that lie ahead. People who are not trained or prepared for their performances can lose their audiences.

God is sending us the early rain and the later rain. Only prepared people will benefit from the good things of the land as the rain waters the land for a timely harvest.

Preparation in life is of great value and requires time, effort, and resources. Everything we do takes time and planning. Planning includes a time to wait and prepare for action.

Most of the time, things are not done overnight, except in critical situations. Every day, as we go from place to place, we see people who are not prepared to do things but who do them anyway.

Between you and me, people look stupid when they are on stage to do something they did not prepare for. It actually makes them simple. I do not want to do that. Do you?

It is important for us to prepare for something before we engage in it.

Inadequate preparation always leads to bad implementation; bad implementation leads to terrible results.

In the final analysis, forfeiture, dismissal, loss, and sorrow can be the results. Is that what you really want? Why not wait and prepare accordingly?

If preparation is that important, why are many people jumping the turnstiles instead of waiting in line? Again, as I said in the beginning, society has taught us to move forward in life, but rarely tells us to be patient and wait for our time.

When we overlook the time required to wait and prepare for a person, place, or thing, we tend to jump ahead of those things. When this happens, instead of being at the front of the line or on stage, we find ourselves in the back of the line or sometimes thrown out of line altogether.

I have seen young people rush through life; many times, it leads to disaster. I see people rush into relationships without a second thought. Sadly, the pain and turmoil they later experience outweighs the initial emotions, leaving them with broken hearts and, sometimes, plenty of trouble.

Some people who rush into business will crash before they kick things off because they have no foundation. They overlook preparation, and when reality sets in, they are devastated.

I have seen pastors rush into ministry, leaving their seniors without appointment and blessing. Before they know it, the little fire and fame carries them into the abyss of short-lived dreams and destruction.

When we do not prepare for the challenges that lie ahead of us, we will fail. A lot goes into preparation, such as planning, time, materials, people, and money. Those who think that life can go on without preparation will face disappointment.

When we fail to plan, we plan to fail.

Life demands preparation. Brides must prepare for their bridegrooms. Students must prepare for examinations. At red lights, drivers must prepare for full stops.

Surgeons must prepare their patients for surgery. Athletes must prepare in practice before their big games. Pastors must prepare their messages before they preach. In a general election, the winner must be prepared for the presidency. Even NASA must prepare its rockets for take-off and landing. Preparation is essential.

Why do people want to go through life without preparing themselves? Without adequate preparation, we can do little or nothing. If we do not prepare, we will not perform correctly.

Life demands preparation. If we want to become what God has called us to be, if we want to take charge of our lives and this world, we must prepare ourselves for the challenges ahead.

Do not rush ahead in life without being prepared, lest you become the first victim. God does not want you to become a negative statistic; rather, he wants you to be a champion. Prepare yourself today; the world is waiting for your jaw-dropping performance.

Chapter 21: Waiting Gives Us Knowledge

When we wait for our time, we gain better knowledge of the place, person, or thing we must engage. Insufficient knowledge is as bad as no knowledge, so learning about what we are getting involved in is of vast importance.

In the military, officers and spies acquire "intel," which is knowledge of the enemy, before making decisions about war. Attacking an enemy stronger than you can be quite devastating, so spies bring must valuable intel to the decision makers before they commit the army to war.

Because this advance knowledge is so important, we are usually given orientation when we start new jobs and other endeavors.

There are times when we must wait patiently; even the mountains before us can move before we take our journeys. Instead of trying to fight the mountains, climb them, or go around them, we must let patience lead the way. We do not have to fight every war; we simply need to wait out some things. God is working on our behalf.

When we wait for God's perfect timing, he can fight for us and make the enemies our footstools in a battle we do not necessarily have to fight.

[111]*Since that time he waits for his enemies to be made his footstool.* [Hebrews 10:13]

Let me ask you a simple question. Do you really want to fight unnecessary battles? I don't think so; I don't. God says that there are times when we must wait so that he can do all the work for us.

We do not have to fight every battle; God himself wants to take care of some things for us. All we have to do is to wait and let God be God. People who do not have this knowledge go on attacking people and things they have no business fighting. As we wait on God, he gives us knowledge of the things he can do on our behalf.

[112]*These all wait for You, that you may give them their food in due season.* [Psalm 104:27]

There are seasons in life; everything happens in its season. Ignorance of the seasons in life—including the season of waiting—could make us lose important things. When we wait for the Lord, he gives us food, housing, a business, family, ministry, health, happiness, and longevity.

Sometimes people betray and hurt us; in these cases, most of us wish to take revenge and make the perpetrators pay for their crimes. However, God says that we must not pay evil for evil. Instead, when we put our trust in him and wait for him, he will save us from loss and pain.

The writer of Proverbs in the Bible admonishes us by saying,

[113]*Do not say, "I will recompense evil"; wait for the Lord, and He will save you.* [Proverbs 20:2]

As we wait for the Lord, the knowledge that God will take care of those who hurt us will prove to be a great help. To know that we do not need to hunt all those who hurt us and that God will bring them to justice is a relief.

If we rush and do not learn all that is available to us, we will fall prey to the elements of life and become victims instead of the leaders whom God has called us to be.

Let us get all the knowledge we need before we proceed in life. We must have proper knowledge so that we can make informed decisions. Let us make sure that we are not ignorant fools or arrogant losers.

Chapter 22: Waiting Instills Character

In life we must have good character and a good reputation. We cannot become people who grow so fast they leave their brains behind. We need integrity; we need character.

The Psalmist said,

[114]Let integrity and uprightness preserve me, for I wait for you. [Psalm 39:7]

Integrity and righteousness should guide our journey in life. These are essential values and not things people get overnight. It takes time and hard work. When we wait for our time in life, we acquire integrity and become upright people for the present and the future.

The psalmist said that,

[115]I waited patiently for the Lord; And He inclined to me, and heard my cry. [Psalm 40:1]

We should not wait in haste, but rather wait patiently for the Lord. We must wait with eagerness and expectation. When we wait for the Lord and for our time in life, God gives ear to our cry and responds to us.

There are times when all we have to say to the Lord is,

[116]Lead me in your truth and teach me, for You are God of my salvation; on you I wait all the day. [Psalm 25:5]

There is a longing in the human soul for something beyond us. We must all search ourselves, slow down, and say,

[117]My soul waits for the Lord more than those who watch for the morning; yes, more than those who watch for the morning." [Psalm 130:6]

When I look at my life, I can truly say that my soul waits for the Lord, more so than those who watch for the morning.

My day is in the Lord; so instead of waiting for the dawn of a new day, I wait on God himself.

Though I am developing myself into a person of character and integrity, I must admit that at times I make mistakes. It is so good to know that in my moments of weakness, God will not stay angry with me forever. The Bible speaks of God in the Psalms when it says,

[118]For his anger is but for a moment, his favor is for life; weeping may endure for a night, but joy comes in the morning. [Psalm 30:5]

My immaturity could make me lose my chance at receiving God's forgiveness for my weaknesses. However, maturity teaches me to have a heart of remorse for my sins and weaknesses, and helps me make things right with God and his people.

I am so thankful to God that he helps me obtain all the tools I need before I jump into things. I need patience. I need to wait for God's perfect timing.

Sometimes it seems like God is late for everything, but I cannot be delusional and have such naive thoughts. I understand that there are rewards when I wait on the Lord. His thoughts and my thoughts do not operate the same way. To be frank, I prefer the timing of God. He is always right.

Chapter 23: Waiting Brings Rewards

It is rewarding to wait for God. One of the best things we can do is to wait for our time because there is a time for everything. Anything short of the appointed time will bring us the wrong things; this is not something we want.

The writer of Lamentations in the Bible tells us that,

[119]*The Lord is good to those who wait for Him, to the soul who seeks him.* [Lamentations 3:25]

God is truly good to those who wait for him, and definitely good to those who seek him. What good is life when we do not have the blessings of God? When we wait for God, it does not matter how many people went ahead of us; when God is good to us, we can outdo all the people who are ahead of us.

The goodness of God surpasses everything in life. When God is good to you, favor finds you. I would rather wait for God's time so that he can be good to me rather than rush into life, leave God behind, and face troubles I cannot handle.

I have come to understand that when I wait on the Lord, he listens to me. No wonder the Psalmist said,

[120]*I waited patiently for the Lord; and he inclined to me, and heard my cry.* [Psalm 40:1]

I want God to listen to all my prayers, tears, complaints, and positions. Waiting for God puts us in a place where he listens to us; I think that is a great blessing.

There are times in life when we really want to get back at those who hurt us. However, it is so good to know that God is not simply about love and forgiveness; he is also the God of justice. God will fight for me. There may be times when I cannot do anything legally or morally to get to those who hurt me, but one thing I know is that God will raise me up. People may laugh at me. They may think that they are big and bad and that I can do nothing. However, in my personal time I will pray for God to take vengeance on all those who fight to destroy me. I believe that the God of justice will stand up for me against my foes. They will not gloat over me forever; oh no, not forever. One day, when God is ready, their laughter will turn into sorrow. One day my time to be happy will come; thank the Lord for my answer. So, if you are like me and people keep hurting you and taunting you, please exercise patience. God will give you justice. In his own time, he will wipe away your tears and deal with your oppressors. One of the rewards we get when we wait for God is justice. That is why our brother Job said,

[121]*Although you say you do not see Him, yet justice is before Him.* [Job 35:14]

There are talents that must be perfected in us. We must be aware of our gifts and learn how to use them properly. After we do this, we must wait for the right moment to march into the world. The Apostle Paul said to the church in Corinth,

[122]*So that you come short in no gift, eagerly waiting for the revelation of our Lord Jesus Christ.* [I Corinthians 1:7]

Why should we wait on God and for our time? There are gifts, talents, and abilities in us that will come out with time. The best comes out of us when we make room and wait for our time.

God does not want us to rush into life ill-equipped for what lies ahead; rather, he wants us to be fortified with every good and perfect gift from above.

We must know one thing: our time of waiting is not time wasted.

Our delay is not our denial.

Life can be difficult. Sometimes people rush and get ahead of us in life. We would like to jump in and move forward in life too, but we must not do so until we have spent time before the Lord, waiting on him. Let those who are ahead be ahead. Our time will come.

The Prophet Isaiah offered some words of consolation when he said,

¹²³But those who wait on the Lord shall renew their strength; they shall mount wings like eagles, they shall run and not be weary, they shall walk and not faint. [Isaiah 40:31]

Let us take comfort in the Lord, knowing that our time seeking and waiting before him is not in vain. It is good to know that the Lord rewards those who wait on him. In our time of waiting before the Lord, we will gain strength. We must rise up and take our proper place in life. It is good to know that we will run our race and not become tired. We will walk and not faint. Many people may go ahead of us, but reality shows us that not all of them keep their pace. A good number of them will fall to the back of the line. It would have been better for them to wait for the Lord's time than to rush and fall flat on the floor. Why rush in life?

People are going to get ahead of us; let them go. When our time comes, some of those people will serve us, so it's okay for them to go ahead now and learn how to be of good service to us. Isn't that simple?

If you are like me, you want good doctors, lawyers, teachers, butlers, chauffeurs, nannies, and gardeners. It is expedient to let some people ahead of you so that they can serve you better tomorrow. Some of these people are actually doing you a favor by getting train so that they can serve in your compound tomorrow. This does not in any way put down all the wonderful people who serve in these various capacities. Certainly not! We need people of expertise in different areas of service. Life would be difficult without them.

However, there are other people who, by rushing ahead in life, crush tomorrow because they are not prepared for the pressure they'll face. When that happens, they will retreat with sorrowful faces, pleading to stick around and do anything.

I cannot overemphasize the importance of waiting on the Lord and seeking him daily; I know it is hard, very hard, but it is worth it.

I want to tell you a little story about our world and our attitudes. In our world today we do not like to wait for anything. We talk before we think. We talk before we realize that the person to whom we just spoke is a chronic gossiper.

We rush to bed with people whose names we don't know without thinking about our compatibility. We make rash decisions before considering the implications and consequences.

We enter business deals before we understand the details of the contracts. We give up on people before they have a chance to hear our message and change, as though we ourselves are perfect.

We go before God in a hurry to get ahead in life without remembering that our current problems have led us to him. And, for some of us, once God answer our prayers, we don't come back until we have other problems. We say short prayers and attend church occasionally, but we expect so many miracles from God.

What more can I say about the trivial subject of patience and waiting? For most of us, our problems stem from the fact that we did not wait for God and our time. We rushed into life without being properly preparing ourselves for the challenges that lie ahead.

Life can be deceptive. It can put us in a trance and give us the delusion that we can simply rush ahead to find everything lined up for us just the way we imagine.

For the most part, we do not get the chauffeurs, butlers, managers, and stewards; what we get is none of the above. I conclude by saying that it is better to wait for God than to have regrets.

Wait for your time. Even those who are close to the right people and their breakthroughs must learn to wait before they get ahead of themselves and mess up things. It is very important that we wait for the right time.

The Apostle Peter needed to wait for his time and place. Interestingly, even Peter was rushing to take a position before his time.

Instead of paying attention to the ministry that Jesus was about to give them, Peter and the other disciples argued over who would be the greatest after Jesus departed. Peter had no idea that during the time they spent arguing, the devil was planning and asking permission from God to utterly destroy him.

Peter still didn't learn; upon the arrest of Jesus, he took his sword and cut off one of the guard's ears. Peter thought that he was ready to fight for Jesus—and to die for him. Yet a few hours later Peter denied Jesus three times before the cock crowed.

He ran away, abandoning the Messiah out of fear and guilt. The same Peter who had been jumping up and down simply couldn't stand the tension; he immediately fled for his life. What a disgrace!

The seventy-two disciples greatly rejoiced upon their return from the first mission trip because the demons had fled from them. However, Jesus told them not to rejoice too early just because a few demons had fled; they had to rejoice because their names were written in the Lamb's Book of Life. Ah, sometimes we celebrate too early!

They had to wait for the appropriate time to rejoice, and it wasn't because a few demons had fled. There were greater things ahead of them—continuing the ministry, being consistent, finishing strong, and receiving the winners' reward in heaven.

They had no idea what real ministry would be. They had no idea how the authorities would chase them all over the place and work overtime to silence them. They did not think about the beatings, jail time, and cruel deaths many of them would face. They just never knew what was ahead of them and they celebrated the casting out of demons too early.

They never understood that though a few demons obeyed them and fled, they needed the Holy Spirit that would dwell in them during Pentecost. Pentecost would come only after Jesus went to the cross and ascended to heaven. The disciples didn't understand how much that experience would cause them to change the world forever.

In time, Jesus died, resurrected, and ascended to heaven; in obedience to his word, the disciples waited in the Upper Room in one accord. As Jesus had foretold, as they prayed they received the empowerment of the Holy Spirit and they busted out in strange languages—the Speaking in Tongues began.

When this happened, the same Peter who had argued about which of them was the greatest, who couldn't pray with Jesus in Gethsemane, who had denied Jesus three times and run away from a little girl—this Peter stood up and preached his first sermon to a large crowd and saved 3000 people!

The 12 disciples, with Peter as their leader, spread out after Pentecost and created a movement known as Christianity. Today it still preaches the gospel message of Jesus Christ of Nazareth. When the disciples received the Holy Spirit—for which they had to wait some time—they became different people and changed the world.

God has something special for you, but you must wait for him. God wants to prepare you. There is something bigger and better ahead of you.

When you and I rush and leave out the important things we need in life, our journey will most likely end up in disaster. Do not get a broken heart; wait on the Lord. Wait!

Wait! When we wait, we get strength and renewal.

Wait! When we wait, we express our trust in God and declare that he knows what is best for us.

Wait! All this could be a test that we must pass to get to the next level in life.

Wait! In our time of waiting, we have the chance to correct our mistakes and fix loose ends before our uplifting.

Wait! There is joy in getting what we have been waiting for. It is an inexpressible joy beyond words.

Wait! Your delay is not your denial.

Wait! There are some important things you need to know, people you need to meet, and other resources you need for your journey.

Wait! There is no need to rush, because when we rush we will fall. It is better to wait for our time. It is far better to wait for God.

Wait!

PART SEVEN:
Connecting the Dots

In this section, we will discuss how we can connect our reality with our dreams and aspirations for life. Simple illustrations will help us discover ways to make the right choices and take the proper steps of faith to reach our destinies.

I understand how great and talented we are as people. I mean, no one can doubt the advance of science and technology and human development. Yet in the midst of these advances, a constant, unquenchable yearning in our souls does not find rest.

As you go through the next pages, open your heart and mind. I believe that the Lord will give you a bridge over your troubled waters.

Chapter 24: You Cannot Do It Alone

At the dawn of creation, it was God who formed man and placed us here. We did not, as many would have us believe, simply emerge from atoms, molecules, and gases that went through successions of evolutional change over millions of years. We were carefully thought out and created by the Chief Designer himself.

God created us. He established our purpose and domain and gave us power to rule all things on land, in the waters, and in the air. God blessed us and told us bear fruit, multiply, fill the earth, subdue it, and have dominion.

Yet some time in history, we blundered and sinned against God. Instead of taking responsibility for our actions, we began blaming one another and accusing God.

The result of our sins and crimes was the lifting of God's power and authority upon us to rule and govern the earth; our choice to do evil heightened. Instead of being in charge, we became victims of circumstance by choice.

Since that time, man has chosen evil over good. The little good we do is always challenged by the constant presence of evil. Many times, we get carried away by the good things that happen around us. We think that the whole world is at peace and is having a fine time.

The ugly truth is that, as we enjoy life here, war, famine, sickness, systematic injustice, poverty, and marginalization are occurring across the globe. As a matter of fact, some of these terrible things are happening in our own cities, yet no one seems to care.

So what do we do? Before I answer that, let me ask you a question. Do you simply care about yourself and your family, or are you concerned about the plight of others? Please keep that in mind as I answer the first question.

I am the type of guy who does not look at the Owner's Manual for anything that requires assembly. I usually open the box and begin to put things together. Sometimes it works; when that happens, I feel so proud of myself.

However, there have been times when, after wasting an hour or two mixing and matching things to no avail, I will sheepishly pick up the

Owner's Manual, follow the instructions, and assemble the stuff. Isn't that stupid?

Hmm. Did you just say yes? Come on! Do not pretend to be perfect. I bet you have done something like that before. It may not be a box of toys, a bicycle, or a computer, but perhaps you should have consulted the Owner's Manual for the last person you dated, your career choice, or the place where you are living.

Ah ha; now you are thinking about how that went; perhaps it was not the best experience. You see, had you checked the Owner's Manual, you would have seen right away how faulty that person or thing was and would not have wasted your time and resources on it.

From the very beginning, the two of you were incompatible. How did you not know? If it was damaged in the box, or faulty in operation, you would have taken it back to the store right away to exchange it or get a refund.

Sadly, you did not know how messed up that person or that thing was and you attached yourself to it. In the end, it was not worth your time, money, and energy. I tell you the truth, this is what most of us do, and it causes us to live our lives in regret. Shamefully, we say, "Had I known," as though we will not do it again.

Please do not try to set up things that require assembly without consulting the Owner's Manual. It is there to help you. Set aside your ignorance, curiosity, and pride; there is no room for those things here. To make life easy, simply pick up the Owner's Manual and follow the instructions.

Where is the Owner's Manual for life and how to govern this world? It is with God. God has the Owner's Manual for your life and your family. He has the perfect fit for your dreams and aspirations.

God has the thing to help you discover your purpose and reach your destiny. He knows the right education, career, spouse, and decisions for you. All you have to do is ask Him to help you. Let me say this: as you ask God to show you the Owner's Manual for your life, you must be willing to trust and obey him.

An interesting fact about God is that He does not simply give away lessons to life without helping us understand what they mean. God is truly a people person.

There is more to God than we know. God has a strong and caring team of customer service personnel standing by to help us understand certain things in the Owner's Manual. These customer service personnel are the angels and the Holy Spirit. They are ready and willing to help, but you must make the call.

Many times, in our stupid pride and ignorance, we do not ask God to help us. This always brings about problems. Whether they are small or large, these unnecessary problems have a way of negatively affecting our lives and preventing us from fulfilling our purposes. We need God.

Chapter 25: We Need God!

I know that, in certain parts of the world, it may sound crazy that are working tirelessly to expel God from their cultures and homelands, but the truth is that the need for God is ever-present. I believe that we need God more now than ever before.

People have become more insolent, wild, and disrespectful of values that have upheld our nations for centuries. People are working overtime to erase any reference to God in public arenas; they are becoming viler than ever. With certain lawyers ready to sue anyone—and now any business—that promotes God in public places, our children will not know about God if we are not careful.

Society has kicked Bibles out of schools and hotel rooms, but has installed them in jails and prisons. What kind of logic is behind this? If Bibles are such good means of helping prisoners come clean that they are guarded by state security officers and funded by money from taxpayers, could their usage not positively affect our students and hotel guests as well? Are we backwards or what?

Homosexuality is permeating our society to the extent that it somewhat overrides proponents of religion and family values. Governments are creating laws to protect homosexuals and, sometimes, to suppress the rights of others.

Western governments are running special campaigns for the homosexual agenda and are telling third-world countries to be gay so that they can receive aid and development money in return. Wow, I think that is ridiculous! How much money do people get for been straight?

Many developed countries now have atomic bombs that are real weapons of mass destruction. Over the years, the AK47 gun has killed more people than did the Hiroshima atomic bomb; yet people still make these killing machines that almost anyone can buy. We must now pray for these countries, that they not get mad and threaten to nuke one another.

Science and technology have advanced so much that people can illegally hack into anything and cause immeasurable damage to governments, banks, retail chains, airlines, and individual bank accounts. Even if the bad guys are caught, the damage seems irreversible. No one is safe these days.

Our families are all at risk. As effective as home security systems are, they can keep away only dull, stupid intruders; not so for the smart ones. Home security systems, especially home video surveillance, will not protect us from smart, wicked computer geniuses. They can use our own security systems to spy on us, divert our calls for help, and harm us; then they can leave without a trace. We are secure only because of the grace of God.

Our families are exposed to many things we do not like. TV has become a problem. TV ratings have changed from G and PG to R and M. Now we have what the world really wants—TV Naked!

From nude beaches to the public media, we can now all be naked and look for men and women on TV. I do not know how to answer our children about this sort of insane exposure. I wonder what has happened to the laws against indecent exposure and lewdness.

We all want freedom and liberty. To be frank, I think the world should recognize that there is a limit to everything. Some things—such as nudity—are just not meant to be seen in public.

Tattoo parlors are booming nowadays because everyone, including believers, wants tattoos all over their bodies to hide their skin colors. If we are not careful, in a short while people will walk around naked in their neighborhoods, wearing nothing but tattoos to cover themselves up.

Instead of beach-watch teams looking for inappropriate bikinis, police will be checking tattoos because the people wearing them are naked!

Human depravity is growing at an alarming rate that will cause irrevocable damage if we are not mindful. In our world today, abortions are normal, even among Christians.

Corruption is a crime only when poor people do it on a small scale; for the rich and powerful, it is not really considered a crime. In their case, the name changes from "corruption" to "embezzlement" or "misappropriation of funds."

Many uneducated people do not know how to pronounce these big words, so they do not say anything at all. If they were to complain, no one would listen because the system marginalizes the poor and uneducated.

Terrorism pervades the world today. But what is terrorism and who defines it? It seems as though we consider an act to be terrorism only when people from certain religious groups do it and when certain people of color do it. When others commit such acts, the mass media refuses to call those acts what they really are—terrorism. In these cases, the media says that the person is mad or has medical problems; it's as though wickedness is only for a certain class and people. It seems as though the world is concerned about terrorism only when it affects the West; in other places, especially Africa, no one seems to care. Some big countries with good-looking people are behind all the terror attacks. They train the militants. They provide the money. They provide the guns and other munitions. Interestingly, they talk about such acts only if they do not like someone in power who opposes their actions and uses the media and their armies to destabilize regions. What many people do not know is that, in many places in the world, terrorism is funded by countries and special interest groups. What a double standard!

Churches are becoming business centers rather than places of worship. Pastors are not treated as men or women of God, but rather as untouchable celebrities.

Instead of preaching and teaching the uncompromised gospel of our Lord Jesus Christ, these pastors water down their messages; they do not talk about sin, holiness, righteousness, and judgment. Most of their sermons are about positive thinking and prosperity, if not miracles. They seem to be life coaches rather than preachers of the word of God.

They do not want to offend people, especially people who support their churches or ministries. Instead of teaching their parishioners to live according to the word of God, and thereby to spend eternity in heaven, they reduce the gospel ministry to a talent show and use grace as a license to sin openly. They abuse the grace of God and lead masses to damnation.

In many churches and ministries like these, the pastors' salaries are higher than their budgets for evangelism and mission. The pastors often take expensive, luxurious vacations and take church members' hard-earned money to buy things unrelated to ministry. They lack ministerial integrity. Like many others out there, these pastors are immoral. They cover up crimes committed by church members and clergy, and suppress the rights of parishioners.

For them, church is a fanfare, a circus, a show—an easy money-making machine. Because people want miracles, some of these pastors use voodoo and witchcraft and higher satanic powers to produce fake miracles. They know how to brainwash people very well.

Many people have turned away from God because of bad church practices and wicked pastors. Instead of ministering and praying for their members, the pastors take advantage of and prey on them.

I tell you all this so that you can understand the depravity of man and his rejection of God. People are becoming more and more evil every day and are developing more ways to harm others than ever before.

I bring all this up to say that, in the midst of everything, the need for God is constant. We need God. You need God. I need God. Our world today needs God. Things were far better when we gave God his proper place in society. Not that there was no evil then; no. However, people were more conscious of good and evil and morality in the past than they are today.

Are you tired of a world that is becoming more godless? Are you tired of the way people treat each other without remorse? Are you tired of social injustice and marginalization? If so, join me.

If you want to see our nations and lives transformed, let us turn to God. We can redeem ourselves. We can initiate a massive exodus from human depravity, lawlessness, and godlessness into a world of morality, good governance, and respect for human dignity.

So what about you and me today? How does all this relate to us? Well, we all need God. The way things are going, we know that life itself will only get more difficult and scary.

To navigate life, let us ask God to help us. Whether or not you believe in God, this could be your chance to try him and see if he is real. I believe that if you try God, you will discover his reality, love, care, and plan for you.

Like the case of the Owner's Manual, let us ask God to help us. He made us and all the people and things around us. He knows how best to use them to bless us and take us to the next level. All we have to do is try God.

It does not matter how long we have known God; we must connect the dots to achieve our dreams and aspirations. God has a unique way of working with each of us on our own levels.

When we call on him—or simply try to do so—he will show up and guide us through the narrow passages of life. He will speak to us, open our minds, and encourage our hearts to do greater things. I know you want to go forward; do not go without God. We all need him.

PART EIGHT:
#Fix_Me_Up

God made us in his image and likeness and gave us power to rule the air, water, and earth, as well as everything in it. In simple words, we were made to rule the air, land, and water. It is no surprise that humans have explored the land, the seas, the air, and, now, deep space.

We are like God in beauty, character, and purpose. God even put the fear of us upon the animals; they have regard for us. We are a little lower than angels, yet the angels are messengers of God who serve us.

We are stewards and leaders in God's wonderful creation. Do not let anybody put you down and call you bad names. You are somebody. You have a special place in life.

You are so special that your DNA, hair, teeth, and blood are all unique; nobody in the world is like you. You are somebody and you have something to give.

Sadly, even though we are blessed and put in charge, we have been corrupted by the evil in this world. Because of this corruption, many of us have not been able to fulfill our purposes. We cannot reach our destinies.

Our minds perform poorly. We think and talk about useless things at times. We have bad friends, go to the wrong places, and do bad things. If we could go back and fix our minds, thoughts, friends, and activities, as well as the places we go, we would better fulfill our purpose in life.

Looking back at my life today, I know that I need to move forward. I think you need to move forward.

I want to be a good son, a wonderful husband, a loving father, and a prolific writer to inspire my readers. I want to be a powerful pastor and a great community leader. That is why I ask God to Fix_Me_UP! Oh God, please Fix_Me_UP! What about you, my dear?

I want God to fix up my brothers and sisters and all my friends around the world. I want God to fix up all my readers and fans.

My life is not what it should be. I know that you have your own story, too. I believe that I have great potential. I am unique and indispensable. I am wonderful. In spite of my purpose, character, and beauty, I am not where I need to be. I need help.

When I consider all these things, I can say only one thing to God: Fix_Me_Up. I have tried many things on my own. I have tried many things from other people. Now I have made up my mind to do the one thing that counts. That one thing is to ask God to intervene on my behalf.

I am not a lazy person. I do not blame others for my troubles in life. I am a self-starter. I am gifted and hardworking. I am studious, simple, and humble. Yet despite all these wonderful characteristics, things are not what I want them to be.

I am grateful that I know my purpose and calling in life. I am trying to fulfill my dreams and aspirations. As a son, I want my parents to be proud of me. As a husband, I want a happy wife who honors me. As a father, I want to give my kids the best; I want them to be proud that I am their daddy. As a leader, I want to be a leader of leaders. I want to start viral community development programs that empower people to transform their own neighborhoods. Besides this, as a minister I want to minister the Word with passion, clarity, and simplicity—without compromise, but with power. Oh, I want God to use me!

Nevertheless, despite all these wonderful things about me, I am not where I need to be. I need a network that will uplift me and help me fulfill my vision.

To get where I need to be, I need to change some things, people, and places in my life. Perhaps I need to change some long-held ideologies. Do not get me wrong, however, as I am not ungrateful.

Because of my need to ascend to the next level, I must adjust the way I express my emotions. To keep up physically, I must also adjust my diet and weight. God will not give us anything spiritually that our physical bodies cannot handle.

With that in mind, take time before you kill yourself eating tacos, burritos, and hamburgers, or fufu soup and palm butter rice. You must be healthy and physically fit. I think the gym is calling you.

Chapter 26: I am Not a Mistake

God did not make a mistake when he made me; nor did he make any mistakes when he made you. I may not be like other people, but I am grateful to God for what I am. Life is not what it needs to be; I have a lot to learn, many things to do, many victories to win, and many awards to earn.

There are some things from my past that I carry around with me. I have forgotten some of them, but a few have not totally gone away. In fact, some things and people I cannot forget about; we belong to each other. Yet in the midst of all the good and bad things I have experienced in my life, there are few that I need to work on.

I thank God for all the people in my life. I think that we all should be grateful, but if we must advance, we must adjust. When I look at how enormous such changes are in my life, I realize that I cannot do it on my own.

I have friends, family, and coworkers who offer plenty of advice, yet often this advice does not help me; sometimes it actually confuses me.

Now the question becomes tricky. What should I do and to what degree? It is for this that I must call on the Lord to Fix_Me_Up.

Why do I need God's help? Well, the answer is simple. I cannot do this on my own. I am weak. I am confused. I do not have enough faith. Sometimes I am not sure what my work accomplishes. When I put all these things together, my need for God increases. That is why I call upon God to Fix_Me_Up.

King David of Israel was talking of God and humans when he said,

[124]For you created my inmost being; you knit me together in my mother's womb. I praise you because I am fearfully and wonderfully made; your works are wonderful, I know that full well." [Psalm 139:13-14]

I want you to know that you are not a mistake; I am not a mistake. We are the creations of God and he equipped us for the work at hand.

¹²⁵God blessed them and said to them, "Be fruitful and increase in number; fill the earth and subdue it. Rule over the fish in the sea and the birds in the sky and over every living creature that moves on the ground." [Genesis 1:28]

In simple words, God blessed us and said, Be Fruitful, Multiply, Fill the Earth, Subdue it, and Have Dominion. We are blessed and given charge to govern accordingly.

God blessed us so much that he caused the animals to respect us. The Bible says that,

¹²⁶The fear and dread of you will fall on all the beasts of the earth, and on all the birds in the sky, on every creature that moves along the ground, and on all the fish in the sea; they are given into your hands. [Genesis 9:2]

Wow, that means we must really be cool! This makes me wonder about an old question from Kind David,

¹²⁷When I consider your heavens, the work of your fingers, the moon and the stars, which you have set in place, what is mankind that you are mindful of them, human beings that you care for them? You have made them a little lower than the angels and crowned them with glory and honor. [Psalm 8:3-5]

Again, let me join King David to ask, "What is man?" The Bible says in the book of Hebrews,

¹²⁸Are not all angels ministering spirit sent to serve those who will inherit salvation? [Hebrews 1:14]

Man is a little lower than the angels, yet the angels minister to man; what an awesome mystery. I think that we all must truly understand our value. When we do, we will accomplish all that we are meant to live up to and focus on fulfilling our purpose in life.

It is for this reason that the animals respect us. It is for this reason that the angels serve us. God made us for this and blessed us.

Here is the funny thing, though; with all these wonderful things about us, I as a person do not feel like the person described above. I do know that animals recognize my presence. I believe that there are angels and that they are my servants; I am discovering the call to duty that has been placed upon me.

Nevertheless, I feel inadequate. I do not seem to have the capacity to perform in this unfriendly world.

Please understand that I do not have a wasted life. I am trying to apply faith, work, and prayer. But for many reasons I feel that I have been left behind; I feel that I must become better. More than mere feelings and emotions, I know in my heart that I must fulfill my purpose in life.

When I put all these things together, I am more eager to invite God into my life. I know that I can do more; equally important, I know that I cannot do it on my own, regardless of my human connections. I need supernatural assistance. I think the same is true for you.

My brothers and sisters, let us understand that while we may not be scientists, business tycoons, TV preachers, government officials, or other big shots, we are not second-class humans. We are not mistakes. We have purposes that God will help us find so that we can reach our destiny.

Chapter 27: I Have a Purpose

Everything has a purpose. I have a purpose in life. I am not a *"loser," "drop out," "vagabond,"* or *"waste product."*

I am somebody in the eyes of God. I was created in the image and likeness of God. You are somebody. Do not let anyone bully, insult, or humiliate you in any way.

Regardless of how and where I was born, or my current residence, status, ethnicity, and other human connections, I am somebody. I believe that the God who made me gave me a purpose to discover, a reason to live and profit.

I must acknowledge my family and friends for their positions in my life. However, beyond their assistance, God's hand has been with me all along. Sometimes I do not see the hand of God or feel his presence and power, yet I know in my heart that God is with me.

Whether life is good or bad, I acknowledge that God is there. God is with me. God is alive and well even if He chooses not to show up for me at times. Just because few evils have touched me does not mean that God does not have the power to save me or fulfill his purpose in my life.

I believe that the Lord will find a way to connect with me and establish me in my purpose. I know that some people may be a little ahead of me, but that is okay. I will learn to wait on the Lord until my change comes.

I know that I was born to do something. The Bible says that God said to Moses,

[129] *But I have raised you up for this very purpose, that I might show you my power and that my name might be proclaimed in all the earth.* [Exodus 9:16]

I did not die because of abortion or early in life because I have a purpose that God wants me to fulfill. I now know that,

[130] *Many are the plans in a person's heart, but it is the Lord's purpose that prevails.* [Proverbs 19:21]

I had my own plans for life. I wanted to be a businessman or a medical doctor; instead, I will see what the Lord has turned me into.

We must let the will of the Lord prevail in our lives; if we do, we will go further in life than we expect. God has another business in mind; a business that got you reading this book, a business to help thousands of people around the word maintain hope and find the grace of God.

This business, I believe, is the greatest story of my life today. I thank God that I am doing his will. I pray that God will help you discover your purpose and fulfill it.

There are some things that seem conflicting about the will of God and our freedom to choose our own paths in life. To understand how our passions, talents, gifts, and abilities fulfill the will of God without overriding our ability to choose, we must understand the sovereignty of God.

The Apostle Paul, in speaking to the church in Rome, said,

[131]*And we know that in all things God works for the good of those who love him, who have been called according to his purpose.* [Romans 8:28]

God said to the Prophet Isaiah,

[132]*I make known the end from the beginning, from ancient times, what is still to come. I say, "My purpose will stand, and I will do all that I please."* [Isaiah 46:10]

It is quite interesting that God gives people the vision to see the end in the beginning; then he commissions those people for the job. That is why God can say that he knows the end in the beginning; he knows how to make his purpose stand.

Throughout history, we have seen how people's strengths and weaknesses played a role in God's sovereign plan. I know that it is difficult to understand his plan when we consider life's vices and all the evils committed against the innocent; it is difficult to see how God can use such things for his glory.

Truly, all things work together when God is involved. He is the Master Manipulator and the Ace who connects the dots and does the job correctly. I call him the Great Orchestrator because he makes things happen that no one thinks are possible.

I want to admonish you about having purpose. Not all of the things people do are good. Not every purpose is good. In fulfilling our purposes in life, we must examine whether they are just and moral, as well as of benefit to us.

The Apostle Paul warned the church in Galatia,

[133]*It is fine to be zealous, provided the purpose is good, and to be so always, not just when I am with you.* [Genesis 4:18]

I love it. Purpose is purpose. People who kill others have a purpose—to kill—but that is not what we are talking about. We must all come clean. We must stay moral, be honest, and treat others fairly.

We must ask God to help us. Sometimes life is very unreasonable and things do not line up properly to help us become wonderful performers on the stage of life. Yet in the midst of all this, we must work with God and other people to bring out our best. We are called to be champions.

Everyday life demands that we perform well. Whether on the home front or the battle fronts of government, business, corporate life, and the private sector, we are expected to do something. The audience is not friendly to poor performers; certainly not.

They will boo us off stage if we do not perform well. However, if we give them the performance of a lifetime, they will give us a standing ovation and massive applause.

We must all become better. With pressure from family, friends, and coworkers, life can be tough. We all need the help of God.

Not all of us are messed up and do not know our way out; some of us are working on our dreams and visions.

Some of us can boast about the work of our hands because we have something to show for it; but is that all there is? Could we do better instead of settling for what we've done? There is always an opportunity to grow and advance. There are new territories to explore and more innovations to make in terms of products and services.

If we are local, we can go citywide or nationwide—or even international. If we are international, we can improve on existing products and services or come up with something new and better. There is always room to grow.

Let us ask God to rid our minds of useless and evil thoughts. We are Born to Take Charge. Let us be proactive and not simply busybodies who react to people and things.

Many of us fill our minds with things that do not help us. We must rid our minds of all moral depravity, all evil, and all uselessness so that we can improve our functionality. This is what the Apostle said to the church in Philippi because he wanted the best for them,

[134]Finally, brothers and sisters, whatever is true, whatever is noble, whatever is right, whatever is pure, whatever is lovely, whatever is admirable—if anything is excellent or praiseworthy—think about such things. [Philippians 4:8]

We should not think rubbish. We should not poison our minds with bad images related to smoke and illicit drugs and evil things. We can do better.

If you are the type of guy who keeps looking at boobs and butts and never seems to get satisfaction with the one you have, please change. If you are the type of girl who thinks that every guy with six-pack abs—or who is athletic or tall and masculine—should be in your hands, please stop. You can do better.

If you are the type who thinks about nothing except getting high, please stop frying and polluting your brains. If gangbanging is your job, know that something better is out there.

We should think about things that are true, noble, right, pure, lovely, and admirable. Simply put: we should think about good things that will benefit us and other people.

To the church in Rome the Apostle Paul said,

[135]Do not conform to the pattern of this world, but be transformed by the renewing of your mind. Then you will be able to test and approve what God's will is—his good, pleasing and perfect will. [Romans 12:2]

The Apostle Paul equated knowledge of God's will to the transformation of our minds. When our minds are sober and function properly, we can know the will of God.

The Apostle Paul warned that believers should not do as the world does—polluting the human mind—because it is our greatest gift. Worldly people corrupt their minds with immoral images, drugs, and alcohol. Believers and moral people ought to renew their minds so that they can know and do the will of God.

The will of God is that we prosper and fulfill our dreams and visions for life. It is that we have great families and success at work, whatever our work may be.

As we work on our minds, we must work on our hearts before we are deceived. God spoke to Moses about the Jewish people when he said,

[136]*Oh, that their hearts would be inclined to fear me and keep all my commands always, so that it might go well with them and their children forever!* [Deuteronomy 5:29]

Our hearts and minds must work together so that we can be our best. With our minds, we think and rationalize; with our hearts, we sense, know, and judge things.

When our hearts and minds work together, we apply passion to our thoughts. That is what God was speaking about when he told Moses that Israel's heart needed to incline so that it feared him and kept his commands.

I am left to wonder what our world would be like if parents were good to their kids. Parents should give their kids a good, moral upbringing and not depend on schools and the courts to raise their children. It is the responsibility of parents to train their kids. Why are we hurting them?

Our world will be a better place when married couples remain faithful to each other and keep their vows instead of cheating, lying, and hiding dangerous secrets. Cheating hurts; lying is painful. Couples must be truthful and support each other. Love is wonderful. Why do many people do the thing in bed without true feelings just to please their wild libidos? It is totally wrong to pretend to be something we are not just so we can use others and ruin their lives. What if we were the victims; how would we feel?

I think it will be a better world when companies pay employees their correct wages and retirement packages instead of defrauding them. Unions cheat employees after those same employees made the unions rich; poor workers without good lawyers go without benefits. This is so terrible. Why do the rich always cheat the poor? We must all be fair.

I think our world will be a better place when the justice systems administer justice without prejudice, discrimination, and compromise. Peace will prevail when we can trust the courts and law enforcement agencies. Who can we trust to handle our matters nowadays?

Our world will be a better place when we can trust our learning institutions to do their jobs in molding the young minds of our children and not polluting them.

It breaks my heart when schools today, especially in the western world, promote sex education for minors more than they do other academic activities. In other places, teachers regard schools as banks and free sex centers; they defraud students and sleep with them instead of preparing them to be future leaders.

My country, Liberia, has a serious problem with this. I pray that our government and the people of Liberia will work together to cleanse our learning institutions of corrupt teachers who trade sex and money for grades.

These wicked teachers cheat the students who are not learning anything. They also cheat the students' parents because, even though the parents pay school fees, their kids are not learning anything; this kills the dreams of families.

These criminals cheat the country by robbing it of sound, educated youth who should be the leaders of tomorrow. They ensure that our graduates are ignorant fools ill-equipped for today's workforce. These students do not stand a chance in the modern, fast-paced world.

Corrupt teachers cause problems in the work world because they produce unqualified job candidates who cannot perform required duties. May God help Liberia rid its schools of corrupt and wicked teachers.

Our world will be better if we properly take care of our disabled and elderly people; they are people with equal rights. Let the abuse of our old folks stop.

Many families neglect the elderly and disabled by leaving them in nursing and group homes across the country. Sadly, when the person dies, the family is all too ready to fight over life insurance money.

These people forget that they, too, will get old someday; they will reap what they sow. They forget that when you treat your parents poorly, your kids—who learned from you—will eventually treat you even worse.

When I reflect on these things, I want to spend more time praying and finding ways to create social change. I want to initiate change that will foster growth and development and that will build human capacity. I want to promote a society in which we have respect for human dignity. I believe that we all can ask God to fix us up so that we become better people.

Some of us have a lot to fix because we are far behind, but God knows how to do the job. Wherever we find ourselves, we still have room for improvement. I think that we all need to say, one by one: "God, Fix_Me_Up!" We all have issues; a little divine intervention would do us good.

I want God to help fix my mind, my thoughts, my feelings, and my emotions. I want God to fix everything that is wrong about me. That is why I am very serious about become better. I know I have a great future ahead of me.

I have great potential. I know that I can make my parents proud. I can make my wife happy and be the greatest dad to my kids. I know that. I know that I can be a better minister, a better leader, and, of course, a better writer. And, yes, I know that God can make you better, too. For all these reasons and everything in between, I pray this simple prayer everyday: "God, please Fix_Me_Up!"

Let me be frank with you. Life is not easy. I do not know all that you are facing right now, but I stand with you because we are now one family. If you do not mind, you can ask the Lord to help and fix you up. Let that be your prayer today. I know you can do better. I know I can do better. The Lord be with you. We are in this together.

Chapter 28: Take Charge

If the Bible tells the truth about God—his existence, purpose, creation, and our place in this world—then I must better organize myself. Even if I do not believe in religious jingles and empty rhetoric that sound like rubbish to me, I can try God; if he fails, as I would expect, I have nothing to lose.

However, if God is real and everything about him the Bible states is true, then I must put myself together so that I fulfill my purpose in life. I do not want to miss out on the truth by letting my own deceptions and human inventions lead me astray for eternity.

If I believe only in mere morality without religious underpinnings, in science, in animism, or just in myself and nothing else—if it happens that God is false and that millions of worshippers are hallucinating schizophrenics—I can still go back to my way of life and belief.

All I have done is to prove God wrong—that he does not exist. I have also proven to the millions of worshippers—whether Christians, Muslims, Buddhists, or Hedonists—that they are wrong as well.

The saying will then become true that religion preys on the poor and faint-hearted, that it is not for great thinkers or the affluent. God is totally irrelevant. People who still want to believe in religion do so only to acquire wealth or selfishly promote other causes under that banner.

Whether or not God is false should not matter all that much. I can still learn something from Jesus Christ of Nazareth about vision, organization, training, growth, expansion, passion, sacrifice, and hope.

All these attributes make life wonderful. They are useful for personal growth, community leadership, government, business, the non-profit world, and every discipline of life. These attributes teach us how to properly use resources so that we get what we envision.

They teach what businesspeople call customer service because they involve delivering goods, products, and services with the customer at heart.

I know that some of you are already wondering what this has to do with taking charge; oh yes, it has everything to do with our ability to take charge.

Before, during, and after Christmas, non-Christians profit so much from the Jesus they do not believe in, earning huge profits in sales. Businesses worldwide have seen that, in many places, they earn their highest profits at Christmastime.

They do not believe all that religious stuff, but they cash in heavily on the Jesus of Christmas; for many, Christmas is the best thing that happened to their businesses.

Now let me ask you a simple question: to you, who is this Jesus Christ of Christmas from whom the world profits? If non-religious people know how to profit from Jesus, what about Christians who know Jesus as their personal Lord and savior?

Must they wait for Christmas or can they benefit from Jesus every day, from his love, acceptance, forgiveness, hope, healing, deliverance, breakthroughs, and many other miracles?

I think the answer is a simple yes; Christians should do more than benefit from Jesus; they should recognize his lordship and give him surrendered lives and proper worship.

Now that we have gotten this out of the way, let us discuss the topic of taking charge. If we have God, Jesus, and the host of heaven on our side, yet unbelievers seem to benefit so much, we must Take Charge of our lives and ask God to fix us so that we can be established in him.

In the physical world, it would not be good if strangers, neighbors, and others enjoyed the money and property of my father while I, as a son, had no special place. If I have to struggle and fight my way in line for a ration from my own father, who am I?

No way; that would not be cool at all. I should be the one to help the needy. I should not be one of the needy standing in line to profit from my father when I am his son.

When it comes to God, he is our father and we have all the rights and privileges of sons and daughters. We should not be treated like strangers or beggars. Unfortunately, many of us are way back in line waiting for rations when God is our father. We must wake up from our slumber; arise, shake ourselves, and take our proper place in the Lord.

We must remember that, in Genesis, we are told that we are made in the image and likeness of God and have been given the power and authority to govern creation.

In addition, we have been blessed and given a charge to Be Fruitful, Multiply, Fill the Earth, Subdue It, and Have Dominion. As a matter of fact, as a way of helping us believe in ourselves and recognize his sovereignty, God caused the animals to respect us.

With this call to tend and care for creation, blessed and commissioned, why should I not be one of the known stewards, managers, and overseers who shake and move things?

Why do I find myself in the back of the line, struggling to get rations? This reminds me of a story Jesus told in the Bible. It's called the "The Parable of the Lost Son." Here it is.

[137] *Jesus continued: "There was a man who had two sons. The younger one said to his father, 'Father, give me my share of the estate.' So he divided his property between them.*

"Not long after that, the younger son got together all he had, set off for a distant country and there squandered his wealth in wild living. After he had spent everything, there was a severe famine in that whole country, and he began to be in need. So he went and hired himself out to a citizen of that country, who sent him to his fields to feed pigs. He longed to fill his stomach with the pods that the pigs were eating, but no one gave him anything.

"When he came to his senses, he said, 'How many of my father's hired servants have food to spare, and here I am starving to death! I will set out and go back to my father and say to him: Father, I have sinned against heaven and against you. I am no longer worthy to be called your son; make me like one of your hired servants.' So he got up and went to his father.

"But while he was still a long way off, his father saw him and was filled with compassion for him; he ran to his son, threw his arms around him and kissed him.

"The son said to him, 'Father, I have sinned against heaven and against you. I am no longer worthy to be called your son.' "But the father said to his servants, 'Quick! Bring the best robe and put it on him. Put a ring on his finger and sandals on his feet. Bring the fattened calf and kill it. Let's have a feast and celebrate. For this son of mine was dead and is alive again; he was lost and is found.' So they began to celebrate.

"Meanwhile, the older son was in the field. When he came near the house, he heard music and dancing. So he called one of the servants and asked him what was going on. 'Your brother has come,' he replied, 'and your father has killed the fattened calf because he has him back safe and sound.'

"The older brother became angry and refused to go in. So his father went out and pleaded with him. But he answered his father, 'Look! All these years I've been slaving for you and never disobeyed your orders. Yet you never gave me even a young goat so I could celebrate with my friends. But when this son of yours who has squandered your property with prostitutes comes home, you kill the fattened calf for him!'

"'My son,' the father said, 'you are always with me, and everything I have is yours. But we had to celebrate and be glad, because this brother of yours was dead and is alive again; he was lost and is found.'" [Luke 15:17-31]

I love this story told by Jesus to deliver a particular message. I love the part that talks about the son coming to his senses. To Take Charge of my life, I must come to my senses. To Take Charge of your life, you must come to your senses.

Though parents worry about their rebellious children, they believe that the kids will come to their senses one day. It is the kids who must make the decision.

God wants us all to come to our senses and see the good plan he has for us. He wants to establish us and promote us, but we must come to our senses and take charge of our lives.

I love the humility of the son when he said, "I will go back to my father and make an apology and also have him give me a condition to show how serious I am about what I am saying."

Let me say this to you who have struggled or who still struggle. When you make up your mind to face the facts of your situation, to deal with them and make restitution to all those you owe, God will help you.

When people see the honesty in you, they will believe in and accept you again, hoping that you will do better this time.

I want to challenge you to go back to all the people you let down and talk with them. Apologize for what you have done and return (or pay for) what you took. Restore any broken relationships to a workable standard.

I want to warn you ahead of time: just because God forgave you does not mean that other people will forgive you, especially after all the bad things you have done. It takes time, diligence, and hard work to restore broken relationships. Do not be pushy and accuse your victims of being unreasonable if they need time to think things through.

If you were in their case and hurt that much, you might not let the culprit off so easily. You might not even forgive the culprit. With that in mind, be patient. The process takes times.

This brings me to the subject of the big brother who was the good son. It is true that he was good. He worked hard every day. But he was wrong to tell his father how and on whom to spend his money. Besides, who was stopping him from throwing his own party, since he had everything? I bring this up to defend those of us who were not doing so good and made dumb mistakes.

Why is it that when we begin to improve our lives and show our worth, naysayers and gossipers—especially friends and families—chew our names around town? Should they not be happy that the Lord has restored us? Why should the stories of our lives be their bread and butter? It is not fair.

Instead of rejoicing that we are improving our lives, they become jealous because they are intimidated by us. When you face these things, do not shrink back; consider it publicity, whether wanted or unwanted. Equate the situation to a celebrity gossip magazine of which you are the star. Meanwhile, be careful that you don't give them reason to tarnish your reputation and destroy your good work. You come from afar; guide this with your life.

In the end, the father called the servants to clean up his son. The father gave the young man his ring of authority and the servants put a beautiful robe on him. Then they threw a wonderful party.

I say this to you: all those who are doing well, continue to do so. Please do not be jealous when you see others improving their lives. Instead of talking bad of them, throw your own party! Be part of the welcoming crew to orient those who have just joined the team.

Take Charge of your life. Run with your vision. Do not let little things get you off balance. Know yourself because you come from afar and have a long way to go.

As I talk about this, I'm brought to another story, "The Parable of the Lost Coin." It is a story in which a lady loses something of value, finds it, and rejoices with her neighbors.

[138]Or suppose a woman has ten silver coins and loses one. Doesn't she light a lamp, sweep the house and search carefully until she finds it? And when she finds it, she calls her friends and neighbors together and says, "Rejoice with me; I have found my lost coin." In the same way, I tell you, there is rejoicing in the presence of the angels of God over one sinner who repents. [Luke 15:8-10]

The story says that the woman had ten silver coins, yet worried so much because she lost one. I wonder why she worried about just one when she still had nine. Oh, I think I know the answer.

Even though she had ten pieces, one was missing. If she did not find it, she would face more worry should others go missing as well. By the time she realized that her coins were gone, it would be too late to recover them.

To save the day, she found a lamp and swept the whole house. The joy of finding this one coin led her to involve the neighbors in a celebration; she was excited about finding it.

This last part says that God and the angels in heaven rejoice over the repentance of one sinner. Well, how important is the repentance of one sinner when there are millions of unrepentant sinners?

God saves nations, cities, villages, and families; he surely takes in one sinner at a time. Whether we approach as groups or individuals, we are all welcome in the kingdom of God.

It is not about repentance alone; it is about taking charge of our lives, of ceasing our non-performance or poor performance so that we live meaningful lives of purpose.

When we take charge of our lives, even our facial expressions express it. The way we dress, talk, think, and relate to others can change. The way we apply our faith, work, and prayer can change. The difference in our persona is evident. People everywhere can sense, see, and hear that we are not *"losers," "drop outs," "useless,"* and *"nobodies."* We have now taken charge of our lives and become *"somebody."* People can count on us to play a meaningful role in this world. We have left the spectator bench and entered the arena of qualified performers.

When our performance is good, our parents are proud that we belong to them, our spouses are honored to be married to us, our children call us wonderful, and the community counts on us. The government recognizes us, and the church is surely blessed because of us. We are not simply bystanders anymore.

We will be the movers and shakers of society. All this happens when we take charge. It goes from "mine" to "ours."

Life goes from selfishness to selflessness.

It now considers the interest of others and not simply our interests alone. When we take charge of our lives, we take care of our environment; we conserve, replenish, and sustain the planet.

When we take charge, we get ahead in life. We have freedom from all the little anthills that looked like humongous mountains. When we take charge, we become champions. We sacrifice for our own and stand the test of time.

When we take charge of our lives, we become innovative and improve on existing things and ideologies. We also become creative, giving birth to new and better things. When we take charge, we let others win at times so that all of us can chant the victors' song.

The world needs us. The stage is set. The arena is jam-packed. The spectators are chanting. The only missing piece of the puzzle is us. It is you. It is me. Come on, my brother; come on, my sister. Arise and plug it in.

Arise and take charge of your life now; if you do not, no one will do it for you.

Arise and take charge of your family; it is the best gift you have.

Arise and take charge of your work, it is your means of survival and recognition.

Arise and take charge of your community; you need people, and people need you.

Arise and take charge of your nation; leadership calls.

Arise and take charge of the church; the Lord is watching.

Arise, arise, arise; arise and take charge; you do not have enough time.

Arise and take charge because you were Born to Take Charge! Take charge!

If you don't mind, I want you to drop everything now and talk to God about your situation. I do not know what you are going through, but I believe that the Lord is waiting for you to take charge of your life.

Start with a simple prayer and ask God to help you take charge of your life, your feelings, your thoughts, your friends, the places you go, your work, your business, your church, your ministry, your relationship, and any other thing that comes to mind.

Just ask God to help you take charge of everything. Remember, you were created and born to do this. God already blessed you and commanded you to bear fruit, multiply, fill the earth, subdue, and have dominion. Declare it now.

You are not a loser. You are not a dropout. You are not useless. You are not good for nothing.

You were born to be a great leader. The world is waiting for people like you to make a difference. Go on, do your thing. Stick your signature on it. Let your style flow. Let people know your name. The world is waiting. Go on and take charge.

Take charge and change the world. The world is waiting. Take Charge!

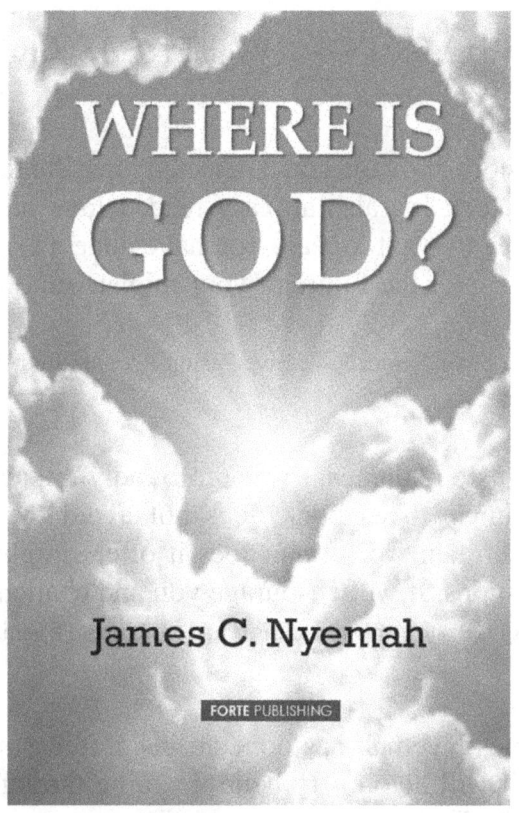

Often, when life hits hard or we drop the ball, we tend to ask, "Where is God?" A most difficult question no doubt but a necessary one about God and life. If things are worse, we even go further and ask all sorts of questions. For example, "If God is such a loving and caring father, why does he allow bad things to happen to good people, including Christians? Why do Christians experience evils as those who are not Christians? Is there a God- one who is Almighty, All Powerful, All Knowing, and All Present God? If so, why do bad things happen to good people? And many more. At these times, we may lose our sense of security in health, in wealth, and in human relationships. They make us doubt the very existence of God, His love and care. We tend to feel that God must be 'picky-and-choosy'. He blesses some people but let the others die in their suffering. We seek resolutions to these questions? We ask of ourselves why He allows these things to happen. This is human Join Rev. James Nyemah as he discusses these tricky, tough questions in, Where is God?

Reviews for "Where is God?"

"I love the story and how you connected your life to it. The number of pages is perfect; it's also an easy read. I love the title. The title will draw people to want to read. You have done a great job. We pray God's blessings over the future of your ministry and this great book. Thanks."
--- Pastor Dale Lane, Senior Executive Pastor, Phoenix First Assembly

"As a classmate of James, I was profoundly impacted by his faith and encouragement. This book does not avoid the harsh realities of living in a broken world, nor does it offer simplistic answers to important questions. It will encourage you and challenge you."
--- Scott Savage, Pastor of Spiritual Formation, North Phoenix Baptist Church

"Pastor James Nyemah has done an insightful work on this book and I believe it will help every believer going through the storms in life to be hopeful."
--- Pastor Ezekiel Ojo, Solid Rock Phoenix

I encourage you to watch out for my next book:

"THE POWER OF THOUGHT"

This is a work about how the proper control and usage of our thoughts can help us get the most out of life.

PART 1: The Human Brain and the Human Mind
This part deals with philosophy, science, and religion while elaborating on our good and evil thoughts.

PART 2: The Human Heart
This part presents the heart of man as a Reservoir of Thoughts, but underscores the vitality of Speaking From the Heart. It also warns us about the danger of Unprocessed Thoughts.

PART 3: The Power of the Tongue
This part provides insight on the tongue as a Giver of Life and Death and teaches us about a Tamed Tongue.

PART 4: Doing Our Thoughts
This part articulates the idea of Discerning Thoughts—thoughts about Self, Others, and God.

PART 5: Power of Imagination
This part states, "It's All in your Head!" You can create a real world from a virtual world.

I believe that this book will help you develop and control the "Power of Thought" within you so that you can become your best. There is a champion inside of you waiting to come out. Let us move to a new level of productivity and maturity. Are you ready to move up? I am ready.

VISIT ME ONLINE.

Interact with me and ask questions about my books or whatever else you want to discuss. You can invite me to speak at a small or large meeting; I will be glad to join you.

www.jamesnyemah.com
Follow me on Social Networks:
James Nyemah
Google - YouTube - Facebook **- Pinterest**
Instagram **- Twitter - Tumblr**

BOOK REVIEWS:

"In plain language, Rev. James C. Nyemah challenges all of us to admit our human weaknesses, surrender to God, and through his enablement take charge of our lives to fulfill our God-ordained purposes. Take the chance to read the first page and you will not stop until you read the last sentence."
--- Rev. Jimmy Kuoh – General Superintendent Emeritus, Assemblies of God, Liberia

"This book will touch many lives. The issues addressed are practically what many go through in life. Rev. James Nyemah generously shares outstanding insight and accumulated wisdom and provides a great apologetic for the Bible."
--- Dr. Eric Minta – Christian Hope Ministries Int'l Church

"This is a very good book that young people and adults will benefit from. Take time to read it."
--- Pastor Hypolite Kayenda-muntu – Ramah Full Gospel Church

"Pastor James Nyemah is a good example to follow. He is a leader among many. He united the African pastors in Arizona and organized prayer meetings for the Ebola Crisis in West Africa. We can see from this book no matter what happens in life, you are BORN TO TAKE CHARGE. Read the book and your life will never be the same."
--- Pastor Antonio Kabamba – Jesus Promotion Church International

"This books tells us that we have been given a great gift from God. We must cherish it with ourselves and live a life with purpose. Each journey we take in life has a curve; it is up to each of us to seize every opportunity and make a difference."
--- Ms. Henrietta Andersson – Executive Board Member, Liberia Association of Arizona

"There is no need to remain where you are. Being born proves that there is life. Let the life you live be the expressed purpose by which you were created. It is time to be taken from being a parked car along the curb of disappointment and failure and on to the highway of responsibility in the face of obstacles. Let this book move you to the place of fulfillment in Christ while you take your rightful place in leading others down the way the Almighty God will have them go."

--- Pastor Lonny Du Four – Liberty Tabernacle Ministries

BIBLIOGRAPHY
(Endnotes)

1 Genesis 1:26-28 Holy Bible, New International Version, 1982 by Thomas Nelson, INC, Nashville, Tennessee – USA

2 Genesis 9:2 Holy Bible, New International Version, 1982 by Thomas Nelson, INC, Nashville, Tennessee – USA

3 John 1:16 Holy Bible, New International Version, 1982 by Thomas Nelson, INC, Nashville, Tennessee – USA

4 I Corinthians 12:9 Holy Bible, New International Version, 1982 by Thomas Nelson, INC, Nashville, Tennessee – USA

5 John 1:13 Holy Bible, New International Version, 1982 by Thomas Nelson, INC, Nashville, Tennessee – USA

6 Lamentation 3:22-23 Holy Bible, New Living Translation, copyright ©1996, 2004, 2007. Used by permission of Tyndale House Publishers, Inc., Carol Stream, Illinois 60188.

7 II Samuel 11:1-16,27 Holy Bible, New International Version, 1982 by Thomas Nelson, INC, Nashville, Tennessee – USA

8 Ecclesiastes 3:1 Holy Bible, New International Version, 1982 by Thomas Nelson, INC, Nashville, Tennessee – USA

9 Psalm 4:8 Holy Bible, New International Version, 1982 by Thomas Nelson, INC, Nashville, Tennessee – USA

10 Proverbs 3:24 Holy Bible, New International Version, 1982 by Thomas Nelson, INC, Nashville, Tennessee – USA

11 Matthew 13:24-30 Holy Bible, New International Version, 1982 by Thomas Nelson, INC, Nashville, Tennessee – USA

12 John 10:10 Holy Bible, New International Version, 1982 by Thomas Nelson, INC, Nashville, Tennessee – USA

13 Isaiah 60:1 Holy Bible, New International Version, 1982 by Thomas Nelson, INC, Nashville, Tennessee – USA

14 Proverbs 6:9-11 Holy Bible, New International Version, 1982 by Thomas Nelson, INC, Nashville, Tennessee – USA

15 Matthew 26:39-41 Holy Bible, New International Version, 1982 by Thomas Nelson, INC, Nashville, Tennessee – USA

16 Deuteronomy 9:12 Holy Bible, New International Version, 1982 by Thomas Nelson, INC, Nashville, Tennessee – USA

17 Genesis 27:35 Holy Bible, New International Version, 1982 by Thomas Nelson, INC, Nashville, Tennessee – USA

18 Job 15:35 Holy Bible, New International Version, 1982 by Thomas Nelson, INC, Nashville, Tennessee – USA

19 Genesis 27:40 Holy Bible, New International Version, 1982 by Thomas Nelson, INC, Nashville, Tennessee – USA

20 Psalm 26:4 Holy Bible, New International Version, 1982 by Thomas Nelson, INC, Nashville, Tennessee – USA

21 Luke 19:5-7 Holy Bible, New International Version, 1982 by Thomas Nelson, INC, Nashville, Tennessee – USA

22 Proverbs 1:32 Holy Bible, New International Version, 1982 by Thomas Nelson, INC, Nashville, Tennessee – USA

23 I Samuel 15:22 Holy Bible, New International Version, 1982 by Thomas Nelson, INC, Nashville, Tennessee – USA

24 2 Peter 1:3 – Holy Bible English Standard Version

25 Joshua 22:5 Holy Bible, New International Version, 1982 by Thomas Nelson, INC, Nashville, Tennessee – USA

26 Joshua 22:5 Holy Bible, New International Version, 1982 by Thomas Nelson, INC, Nashville, Tennessee – USA

27 Zechariah 3:7 Holy Bible, New International Version, 1982 by Thomas Nelson, INC, Nashville, Tennessee – USA

28 Luke 11:33 Holy Bible, New International Version, 1982 by Thomas Nelson, INC, Nashville, Tennessee – USA

29 2 John 1:6 Holy Bible, New International Version, 1982 by Thomas Nelson, INC, Nashville, Tennessee – USA

30 2 Timothy 1:6 Holy Bible, New International Version, 1982 by Thomas Nelson, INC, Nashville, Tennessee - USA

31 Matthew 9:17 Holy Bible, New International Version, 1982 by Thomas Nelson, INC, Nashville, Tennessee – USA

32 Deuteronomy 5:33 Holy Bible, New International Version, 1982 by Thomas Nelson, INC, Nashville, Tennessee – USA

33 2 Corinthians 10:6 Holy Bible, New International Version, 1982 by Thomas Nelson, INC, Nashville, Tennessee – USA

34 Deuteronomy 28:1 Holy Bible, New International Version, 1982 by Thomas Nelson, INC, Nashville, Tennessee - USA

35 Romans 8:28 Holy Bible, New International Version, 1982 by Thomas Nelson, INC, Nashville, Tennessee – USA

36 Romans 12:2 Holy Bible, New International Version, 1982 by Thomas Nelson, INC, Nashville, Tennessee – USA

37 Romans 11:13 Holy Bible, New International Version, 1982 by Thomas Nelson, INC, Nashville, Tennessee – USA

38 Ephesians 5:15 Holy Bible, New International Version, 1982 by Thomas Nelson, INC, Nashville, Tennessee – USA

39 Job 24:12 Holy Bible, New International Version, 1982 by Thomas Nelson, INC, Nashville, Tennessee – USA

40 Job 19:25 Holy Bible, New International Version, 1982 by Thomas Nelson, INC, Nashville, Tennessee – USA

41 Psalm 30:5b Holy Bible, New International Version, 1982 by Thomas Nelson, INC, Nashville, Tennessee – USA

42 Proverbs 23:7, Holy Bible, King James Version,1976 by Thomas Nelson, INC, Nashville, Tennessee – USA

43 Romans 12: 1-2, Holy Bible, New International Version, 1982 by Thomas Nelson, INC, Nashville, Tennessee – USA

44 Genesis 6: 4-6 Holy Bible, New International Version, 1982 by Thomas Nelson, INC, Nashville, Tennessee – USA

45 Psalm 94:11 Holy Bible, New International Version, 1982 by Thomas Nelson, INC, Nashville, Tennessee – USA

46 Psalm 55:2 Holy Bible, New International Version, 1982 by Thomas Nelson, INC, Nashville, Tennessee – USA

47 Psalm 55:2 Holy Bible, New International Version, 1982 by Thomas Nelson, INC, Nashville, Tennessee – USA

48 Psalm 10:4 Holy Bible, New International Version, 1982 by Thomas Nelson, INC, Nashville, Tennessee – USA

49 Hebrews 11:6 Holy Bible, New International Version, 1982 by Thomas Nelson, INC, Nashville, Tennessee – USA

50 Old English proverb

51 Psalm 1:1 Holy Bible, New International Version, 1982 by Thomas Nelson, INC, Nashville, Tennessee – USA

52 I Corinthians 15:33 Holy Bible, New International Version, 1982 by Thomas Nelson, INC, Nashville, Tennessee – USA

53 Matthew 7:16 Holy Bible, New International Version, 1982 by Thomas Nelson, INC, Nashville, Tennessee – USA

54 Genesis 1:1 Holy Bible, New International Version, 1982 by Thomas Nelson, INC, Nashville, Tennessee – USA

55 Genesis 1:26-27 Holy Bible, New International Version, 1982 by Thomas Nelson, INC, Nashville, Tennessee – USA

56 Genesis 1:26-28 Holy Bible, New International Version, 1982 by Thomas Nelson, INC, Nashville, Tennessee – USA

57 Genesis 3:19 Holy Bible, New International Version, 1982 by Thomas Nelson, INC, Nashville, Tennessee – USA

58 Proverbs 10:4 Holy Bible, New International Version, 1982 by Thomas Nelson, INC, Nashville, Tennessee – USA

59 Proverbs 12:27 Holy Bible, New International Version, 1982 by Thomas Nelson, INC, Nashville, Tennessee – USA

60 Matthew 7:20 Holy Bible, New International Version, 1982 by Thomas Nelson, INC, Nashville, Tennessee – USA

61 Matthew 7:18-19 Holy Bible, New International Version, 1982 by Thomas Nelson, INC, Nashville, Tennessee – USA

62 Genesis 1:26-28 Holy Bible, New International Version, 1982 by Thomas Nelson, INC, Nashville, Tennessee – USA

63 Exodus 23:20 Holy Bible, New International Version, 1982 by Thomas Nelson, INC, Nashville, Tennessee – USA

64 John 21:6 Holy Bible, New International Version, 1982 by Thomas Nelson, INC, Nashville, Tennessee – USA

65 Genesis 24:56 Holy Bible, New International Version, 1982 by Thomas Nelson, INC, Nashville, Tennessee – USA

66 Job 15:21 Holy Bible, New International Version, 1982 by Thomas Nelson, INC, Nashville, Tennessee – USA

67 Genesis 26:13 Holy Bible, New International Version, 1982 by Thomas Nelson, INC, Nashville, Tennessee – USA

68 Job 36:11 Holy Bible, New International Version, 1982 by Thomas Nelson, INC, Nashville, Tennessee – USA

69 Psalm 25:13 Holy Bible, New International Version, 1982 by Thomas Nelson, INC, Nashville, Tennessee – USA

70 Genesis 1:28 Holy Bible, New International Version, 1982 by Thomas Nelson, INC, Nashville, Tennessee – USA

71 II Peter 1:3 Holy Bible, New International Version, 1982 by Thomas Nelson, INC, Nashville, Tennessee – USA

72 Psalm 18: 39 Holy Bible, New International Version, 1982 by Thomas Nelson, INC, Nashville, Tennessee – USA

73 Jeremiah 29:11 Holy Bible, New International Version, 1982 by Thomas Nelson, INC, Nashville, Tennessee – USA

74 John 10:10 Holy Bible, New International Version, 1982 by Thomas Nelson, INC, Nashville, Tennessee – USA

75 Isaiah 54:17 Holy Bible, New International Version, 1982 by Thomas Nelson, INC, Nashville, Tennessee – USA

76 Isaiah 45:1 Holy Bible, New International Version, 1982 by Thomas Nelson, INC, Nashville, Tennessee – USA

77 Micah 7:19 Holy Bible, New International Version, 1982 by Thomas Nelson, INC, Nashville, Tennessee – USA

78 I Corinthians 10:11-13 Holy Bible, New International Version, 1982 by Thomas Nelson, INC, Nashville, Tennessee – USA

79 II Corinthians 10:3-6 Holy Bible, New International Version, 1982 by Thomas Nelson, INC, Nashville, Tennessee – USA

80 Genesis 1: 26-28 Holy Bible, New International Version, 1982 by Thomas Nelson, INC, Nashville, Tennessee – USA

81 Psalm 8:5 Holy Bible, New International Version, 1982 by Thomas Nelson, INC, Nashville, Tennessee – USA

82 Proverbs 29:2 Holy Bible, New International Version, 1982 by Thomas Nelson, INC, Nashville, Tennessee – USA

83 Daniel 4:31 Holy Bible, New International Version, 1982 by Thomas Nelson, INC, Nashville, Tennessee – USA

84 Mark 1:22 Holy Bible, New International Version, 1982 by Thomas Nelson, INC, Nashville, Tennessee – USA

85 Matthew 20:25-26 Holy Bible, New International Version, 1982 by Thomas Nelson, INC, Nashville, Tennessee – USA

86 Job 25:2 Holy Bible, New International Version, 1982 by Thomas Nelson, INC, Nashville, Tennessee – USA

87 Genesis 9:2 Holy Bible, New International Version, 1982 by Thomas Nelson, INC, Nashville, Tennessee – USA

88 Daniel 2:38 Holy Bible, New International Version, 1982 by Thomas Nelson, INC, Nashville, Tennessee – USA

89 Isaiah 60:1 Holy Bible, New International Version, 1982 by Thomas Nelson, INC, Nashville, Tennessee – USA

90 Deuteronomy 32:4 Holy Bible, New International Version, 1982 by Thomas Nelson, INC, Nashville, Tennessee – USA

91 Psalm 111:6 Holy Bible, New International Version, 1982 by Thomas Nelson, INC, Nashville, Tennessee – USA

92 Psalm 145:10 Holy Bible, New International Version, 1982 by Thomas Nelson, INC, Nashville, Tennessee – USA

93 Romans 3:28 Holy Bible, New International Version, 1982 by Thomas Nelson, INC, Nashville, Tennessee – USA

94 James 2:14,18,20,26 Holy Bible, New International Version, 1982 by Thomas Nelson, INC, Nashville, Tennessee – USA

95 I Samuel 1:1-20 Holy Bible, New International Version, 1982 by Thomas Nelson, INC, Nashville, Tennessee – USA

96 Matthew 14:2-23 Holy Bible, New International Version, 1982 by Thomas Nelson, INC, Nashville, Tennessee – USA

97 Matthew 6:9-15 Holy Bible, New International Version, 1982 by Thomas Nelson, INC, Nashville, Tennessee – USA

98 Matthew 21:18-21 Holy Bible, New International Version, 1982 by Thomas Nelson, INC, Nashville, Tennessee – USA

99 I Kings 18:1-6-40 Holy Bible, New International Version, 1982 by Thomas Nelson, INC, Nashville, Tennessee – USA

100 Joshua 10:13 Holy Bible, New International Version, 1982 by Thomas Nelson, INC, Nashville, Tennessee – USA

101 Genesis 25:21 Holy Bible, New International Version, 1982 by Thomas Nelson, INC, Nashville, Tennessee – USA

102 Matthew 21:13 Holy Bible, New International Version, 1982 by Thomas Nelson, INC, Nashville, Tennessee – USA

103 Matthew 21:22 Holy Bible, New International Version, 1982 by Thomas Nelson, INC, Nashville, Tennessee – USA

104 Mark 9:29 Holy Bible, New International Version, 1982 by Thomas Nelson, INC, Nashville, Tennessee – USA

105 Romans 8:25 - Holy Bible, New International Version, 1982 by Thomas Nelson, INC, Nashville, Tennessee – USA

106 Psalms 106:13 - Holy Bible, New International Version, 1982 by Thomas Nelson, INC, Nashville, Tennessee – USA

107 Psalms 62:5- Holy Bible, New International Version, 1982 by Thomas Nelson, INC, Nashville, Tennessee – USA

108 Galatians 5:5 - Holy Bible, New International Version, 1982 by Thomas Nelson, INC, Nashville, Tennessee – USA

109 Psalms 27:14 - Holy Bible, New International Version, 1982 by Thomas Nelson, INC, Nashville, Tennessee – USA

110 James 5:7 - Holy Bible, New International Version, 1982 by Thomas Nelson, INC, Nashville, Tennessee – USA

111 Hebrews 10:13 – Holy Bible, New International Version, 1982 by Thomas Nelson, INC, Nashville, Tennessee – USA

112 Psalms 104:27 - Hebrews 10:13 – Holy Bible, New International Version, 1982 by Thomas Nelson, INC, Nashville, Tennessee – USA

113 Proverbs 20:22 - Holy Bible, New International Version, 1982 by Thomas Nelson, INC, Nashville, Tennessee – USA

114 Psalm 25:21 - Holy Bible, New International Version, 1982 by Thomas Nelson, INC, Nashville, Tennessee – USA

115 Psalm 39:7 - Holy Bible, New International Version, 1982 by Thomas Nelson, INC, Nashville, Tennessee – USA

116 Psalms 25:5 - Holy Bible, New International Version, 1982 by Thomas Nelson, INC, Nashville, Tennessee – USA

117 Psalms 130: 6 - Holy Bible, New International Version, 1982 by Thomas Nelson, INC, Nashville, Tennessee – USA

118 Psalm 30:5 - Holy Bible, New International Version, 1982 by Thomas Nelson, INC, Nashville, Tennessee – USA

119 Lamentations 3:26 - Holy Bible, New International Version, 1982 by Thomas Nelson, INC, Nashville, Tennessee – USA

120 Psalms 59:9 Holy Bible, New International Version, 1982 by Thomas Nelson, INC, Nashville, Tennessee – USA

121 Job 35:14 - Holy Bible, New International Version, 1982 by Thomas Nelson, INC, Nashville, Tennessee – USA

122 I Corinthians 1: 7 - Holy Bible, New International Version, 1982 by Thomas Nelson, INC, Nashville, Tennessee – USA

123 Isaiah 40:31 - Holy Bible, New International Version, 1982 by Thomas Nelson, INC, Nashville, Tennessee – USA

124 Psalm 139:13-14 Holy Bible, New International Version, 1982 by Thomas Nelson, INC, Nashville, Tennessee – USA

125 Genesis 1:28 Holy Bible, New International Version, 1982 by Thomas Nelson, INC, Nashville, Tennessee – USA

126 Genesis 9:2 Holy Bible, New International Version, 1982 by Thomas Nelson, INC, Nashville, Tennessee – USA

127 Psalm 8:3-5 Holy Bible, New International Version, 1982 by Thomas Nelson, INC, Nashville, Tennessee – USA

128 Hebrews 1:14 Holy Bible, New International Version, 1982 by Thomas Nelson, INC, Nashville, Tennessee – USA

129 Exodus 9:16 Holy Bible, New International Version, 1982 by Thomas Nelson, INC, Nashville, Tennessee – USA

130 Proverbs 19:21 Holy Bible, New International Version, 1982 by Thomas Nelson, INC, Nashville, Tennessee – USA

131 Romans 8:28 Holy Bible, New International Version, 1982 by Thomas Nelson, INC, Nashville, Tennessee – USA

132 Isaiah 46:10 Holy Bible, New International Version, 1982 by Thomas Nelson, INC, Nashville, Tennessee – USA

133 Galatians 4:18 Holy Bible, New International Version, 1982 by Thomas Nelson, INC, Nashville, Tennessee – USA

134 Philippians 4:8 Holy Bible, New International Version, 1982 by Thomas Nelson, INC, Nashville, Tennessee – USA

135 Romans 12:2 Holy Bible, New International Version, 1982 by Thomas Nelson, INC, Nashville, Tennessee – USA

136 Deuteronomy 5:29 Holy Bible, New International Version, 1982 by Thomas Nelson, INC, Nashville, Tennessee – USA

137 Luke 15:17-31 Holy Bible, New International Version, 1982 by Thomas Nelson, INC, Nashville, Tennessee – USA

138 Luke 15:8-10 Holy Bible, New International Version, 1982 by Thomas Nelson, INC, Nashville, Tennessee – USA

www.ingramcontent.com/pod-product-compliance
Lightning Source LLC
Chambersburg PA
CBHW051923160426
43198CB00012B/2016